D0826183

How To Compromise With Your School District Without Compromising Your Child

A Practical Field Guide For Parents of Children With Developmental Disorders and Learning Disabilities

WITHDRAWN

Donated by

SAN RAMON LIBRARY FOUNDATION
100 Montgomery • San Ramon • California 94583

Copyright © 2004 Gary S. Mayerson

Published by: DRL Books, Inc.
                12 West 18 Street
                New York, New York 10011
                Phone: 212 604 9637
                       800 857 1057
                Fax: 212 206 9329
                www.drlbooks.com

All rights reserved. Permission is granted for the user to photocopy limited quantities of the sample correspondence for instructional or administrative use (not for resale). No other part of the material protected by this copyright notice may be reproduced or used in any form or by any means, electronic or mechanical, including photocopying and recording or by any information storage and retrieval system without prior written permission by the copyright owner.

Book Design: John Eng
Cover Art: Ramon Gil

Library of Congress Control Number: 2004108820
ISBN: 0966526686

Contents

Acknowledgements

This book has actually been in the making for more than seven years. It is the natural byproduct of what I have managed to learn to date from listening to parents and school district functionaries and participating in many hundreds of IEP meetings, administrative conferences, due process hearings, and closed-door settlement negotiations. As much as I might enjoy claiming all the credit, this book would not have been possible without important assistance, both direct and indirect, from a variety of sources.

I received invaluable input from a number of school district attorneys, special education directors, school board members and other functionaries who agreed to speak with me "off the record." For obvious reasons, it is not surprising that each and every one of these sources practically made me swear a blood oath *not* to thank them by name in this book. A promise is a promise. For this reason, a generic (but profound) "thank you" will have to suffice. Thank you all for sharing!

It goes without saying that it is impossible to be an effective advocate by simply spouting statutes and decisional law. It is essential to have a good working knowledge of each child's strengths and deficits, and the special terminology and language that comes with the terrain. I cannot imagine being able to do what we do without being able to learn vicariously from the tireless and heroic work of professionals in the field who are reporting from the trenches. I considered trying to name all of these fine professionals, but concluded that an entire chapter could be devoted to this effort and that even after such an effort, I still would miss someone.

Ironically, parents and parent support groups often provide what may be the most important reference points. Just when we start to believe that we have seen it all, the phone will ring and we will hear a story that leaves us shaking our heads in disbelief. The following week, a package will arrive with audiotapes and documentary evidence supporting exactly what the child's parent told us during the initial intake. Every time we speak with a new family, we learn something new.

Julie Azuma of DRL Books made the publication of this book as painless and professional as could be. Additional thanks are due to Kimberly Fusco for her insightful suggestions and edits, and to John Eng, who further edited and formatted the book. Also, thanks to Ramon Gil for his expressive graphic art and layout for the cover.

Finally, I want to thank my family. Thank you all for giving me the breathing room and encouragement to write this book. When you receive a steaming cup of coffee at midnight, it's the best tasting coffee you will ever have.

G.S.M.

We learn geology the morning after the earthquake.

Ralph Waldo Emerson

Introduction

Why this Book?

For already beleaguered parents of children with disabilities, the process of securing appropriate educational programs and services is a daunting one, often involving a precarious journey through a maze of ill-defined hurdles and minefields. The nation's school districts are under a statutory mandate to tailor educational services to the individual needs of the child. Far too many parents, however, will report that they are at loggerheads with school district administrators who instead are tailoring educational programs to meet the fiscal or administrative convenience of the school district.

To be certain, there are many loving, caring and informed school district administrators who pride themselves on always trying to do the "right thing. Over the years, I have met plenty of school district administrators who would fall into this category. Quite a few actually succeed in their efforts. Some of these school district administrators could even be characterized as heroic.

Unfortunately, school district administrators are only human and even the most well-meaning school district administrator is capable of proposing an inappropriate placement, program or service, or allowing an IEP to proceed on "autopilot." IEP implementation can stagnate or go awry like a runaway freight train unless there is someone firmly at the controls.

What causes the educational train wreck? Sometimes, the culprit will be low expectations, budgetary concerns, excessive caseloads or political pressure from the school board. Other times, conflict will arise because of a "control" or policy issue, or because the school district administrator is ill-informed or worse, ill-tempered or "burned out." It is important for parents to understand the various dynamics that may be at play.

Some years ago, I was struck by the fact that while there are many lawyers and law firms accepting lucrative annual retainers to represent school districts in educational rights disputes, there are relatively few attorneys who are ready, willing and able to properly represent the *children*—the real parties in interest. This is entirely understandable. The subject matter is complicated and constantly evolving, the learning curve is steep, the pay is uncertain and erratic, and the risk of failure can often be catastrophic to the child and the child's family. Let's put it this way—there clearly are easier ways to make a living.

More than two thousand years ago, the warrior-philosopher Sun Tzu wrote in his seminal work, *The Art of War*, that "To win without fighting is best." While some disputes will need adjudication following a full-blown due process proceeding, most disputes can and should be resolved much earlier. Just because peace is not immediately at hand, this does not necessarily mean that a due process battle is inevitable. Often, peace (or at least a workable *détente*) is something that can be cultivated.

Parents wrestling with the impact of a developmental disorder or learning disability already have a serious fight on their hands. While due process litigation sometimes is unavoidable, my personal philosophy is that parents should seek to reach a compromise in those situations where it is reasonable and appropriate to do so and where the child will *not* be adversely impacted. This presents a delicate balance that must be respected. That balance is the origin of the title of this book.

It is not my aim to inundate parents with a "Here Are Your Legal Rights" type review of all the pertinent statutes, regulations and court decisions. The legal standards shift and change frequently and to further complicate things, there are regional distinctions. For example, the standard that is applied to ascertain "appropriate" educational progress in the Fifth Circuit, in practice, is somewhat lower than the standard that is applied in other Circuits. These regional distinctions often prompt parents to pick up and move to states that are more receptive to special education.

Note: For many months now, the House of Representatives and the Senate have been haggling over competing and disparate versions of a bill to "reauthorize" the current IDEA statute, last reauthorized in 1997. With a presidential election looming against the backdrop of the economy and national and international security issues, it is anyone's guess as to whether Congress will act to reauthorize the IDEA statute before November of 2004. Unless and until reauthorized in a different format, the existing IDEA statute automatically will continue in its present form. (See 20 U.S.C. Sec. 1400)

While special legal knowledge certainly can be useful, by the time that special legal expertise and knowledge comes into play, parents already are in the middle of their child's due process hearing. The focus of this book, after all, is to try to help parents *avoid* having to go to due process (an administrative trial presided over by a hearing officer or administrative law judge).

An entirely different and more creative approach is called for if parents have any chance of preempting the need to go to due process. In the chapters to come, I will provide parents with *practical* approaches and strategies that are relatively easy to implement, and to sensitize parents to the various dynamics that motivate school district administrators to take appropriate action. Often, these practical strategies can help parents level what is an uneven, if not entirely one-sided, playing field. These very same strategies also can assist parents to be meaningfully prepared for the situation when, after all is said and done, due process litigation proves to be unavoidable.

Most of the strategies discussed in this book were developed in the context of litigating or advocating on behalf of children and adolescents diagnosed with autism spectrum disorders. These practical approaches, however, are equally transferable to *any* disability. To a large extent, they also transcend the applicable legal standards.

Ultimately, whether from the perspective of the parent or the school district administrator, we must never lose sight of the fact that behind all the evaluations, progress reports, correspondence and IEP meetings, there exists a living, breathing child with unique and individual needs. It also goes without saying that behind each of these children stand parents who have not given up their hopes and dreams. This book is dedicated to those parents.

G.S.M.

When written in Chinese, the word 'crisis' is composed of two characters. One represents danger and the other represents opportunity.

John F. Kennedy

Chapter 1

Why Is There Often So Much Conflict At IEP Meetings?

Parents seeking to secure appropriate and effective special education programs and services understandably are anxious and confused about the process of developing an Individualized Educational Plan ("IEP"). In point of fact, there is a heightened level of anxiety long before parents first approach their local school district or early intervention provider.

Once parents discover that there is something that materially distinguishes their child from typically developing children, the search for answers and effective remediation is something that usually permeates a parent's every conscious and subconscious thought. This is what parents of special needs children normally think about at 2:00 a.m. when they are in bed, staring up at the ceiling.

Even anxious parents, however, tend to place a great deal of faith in what their school district or early intervention provider will recommend. Most parents will presuppose and assume that the school district or other local educational agency will have the special knowledge, expertise and motivation to do whatever may be necessary to help their child.

While the overwhelming majority of school district administrators are caring and compassionate human beings who truly *want* to do the right thing, it usually does not occur to parents that some school district administrators might be following entirely different agendas or political mandates, or that they might not even *know* about or have access to the special expertise that is necessary to be ready, willing and able to do the right thing.

> *For example, it is fundamental that unless school district administrators "know what they don't know," it is difficult for them to identify the child's needs, much less address and remediate them appropriately. This is why prudent school district administrators often will look to outside consultants, so as to be able to access a level of special expertise that very well may not be available "in house."*

Parents often will get a healthy dose of reality at the very first IEP meeting—a meeting that typically involves an entourage of seemingly faceless school district employees providing confusing and sometimes inconsistent written reports that have never been seen before (at least not by the parents).

> *Note: It is not at all unusual for IEP meetings to be attended by more than a dozen school district functionaries. In fact, we have attended IEP meetings that have been "packed" with up to two-dozen school district employees. This kind of setting can be overwhelming for parents. Moreover, to add to the anxiety level, it usually is the case that most of the school functionaries in attendance at IEP meetings have never even met the child whose life and future is being planned for.*

Attending the first IEP meeting can make a parent feel like he or she is being sent to the principal's office, except that at the IEP meeting, there are many more "principals" to contend with.

The first IEP meeting (also called an "ARD," "CST" or "PPT," depending on what state you live in) generally is the first time that parents will hear numerous confusing acronyms and terms being thrown around. Just what is the Leiter-R test? What exactly does a Functional Behavioral Analysis involve? Would it be more appropriate to select the CARS, the ADOS or some other assessment measure to evaluate a child suspected of falling on the autism spectrum? What is the ABLLS assessment and how long does it take to administer? What is the SCERTS model? Special education involves a whole new language, and it can be quite overwhelming.

The speed and pace of most IEP meetings is another big surprise for parents. School district administrators are processing scores, if not hundreds of IEP meetings each year. These administrators rarely plan for the IEP meeting to go more than an hour or so. Many IEP meetings that decide a child's educational plan for an entire *year* will be held in a half an hour or less, about the same time that it takes to run a suit over to the dry cleaners.

Does this kind of approach alarm parents who have been waiting an entire school year to attend their child's "annual review?" You bet it does.

Parents who are ushered out the door after this kind of IEP meeting generally have numerous unanswered questions and concerns. While some parents are fortunate enough to walk out of their first IEP meeting with a sense of relief, satisfaction and closure, many others leave their first IEP experience dissatisfied and frustrated, if not entirely "shell shocked."

It is fundamental that IEP decisions are supposed to be tailored to the individual needs of the child. Under the federal IDEA statute and its statutory mandate to individualize educational programs, IEP decisions are never supposed to be driven by the almighty dollar or inflexible "policies" that prevent or impair the individualization process. In practice, however, financial considerations and administrative policy *often* drive IEP decision-making.

While most school districts will publicly take the *position* at IEP meetings that they do not want to discuss the "cost" issue, many so-called "individualized" IEP recommendations are, in fact, primarily motivated by financial considerations. In point of fact, quite a few IEP recommendations will turn out to be driven by broader *policy* mandates communicated by the local school board. Many school districts readily acknowledge that the parent's request is being rejected because "we [the school district] just don't do *that*."

Parents should never accept any policy-based excuse from a school district. When school district personnel make these kinds of statements (statements that show that the district is preventing the individualization of the IEP), a record should be made.

Sometimes, the school district itself will make the necessary record. One particularly brazen school district group in the Midwest actually had the temerity to put on a conference where one of the scheduled topics was "How to Avoid Parents' Demands for Lovaas." Today, most school district organizations will not be so heavy handed. Today, the same topic probably would be entitled "Building a Legally Defensible Autism Intervention Program." School districts clearly have become more skilled in the art of public relations.

Parents should make every effort to attend school board meetings and to collect information and literature distributed by the school board. Parents need to have their ear to the ground to learn about policies and mandates being invoked in the school district that may be *preventing* the IEP team from truly individualizing the IEP. So when the local school board determines to cut out-of-district placements by 50% across the board, that is the kind of broad policy mandate that will clearly be felt and implemented at the IEP stage.

The problem, however, is that parents rarely are privy to such political considerations. When this kind of situation occurs, parents typically are "blindsided." Rarely, if ever, will school district administrators actually come out and candidly admit that they are acting under pressure from their school board or school superintendent. Where there is evidence that IEP decisions are being fueled by broad policy mandates, parents should make a record in order to expose such inappropriate decision-making.

Usually, the school district administrator fulfilling the local school board's "marching orders" will make efforts to convince the child's parents that other, entirely unrelated factors are at play. Typically, the excuse that the school district will come up with is "we believe that your child does not *need* it ["it," of course, being the service, accommodation or support being requested]."

The annual process of approving the school budget often is a heated and politically charged event that is anxiety provoking for many school district administrators, particularly those who find themselves in charge of the district's special education programs.

Note: Many, if not most, school districts will adopt a new budget on July 1. Knowing when the "old" money runs out and the "new" money comes in often can be helpful in negotiating with the school district over costly interventions.

The annual special education budget often is the subject of an annual *apologia* to the district's taxpayers, who perceive that a disproportionately high percentage of the school budget (i.e. tax dollars) is being earmarked for special education services and programs.[1] School district administrators do not relish having to go to the school board with hat in hand. After all, school district administrators can be terminated from their employment and they often are, turning some special education departments in some school districts into "revolving door" operations. In many of these "administrator *du jour*" school districts, fear rules the day and it is all too easy for administrative paralysis to set in.

School board members, in like fashion, fear the political fallout from increases in property taxes, no matter how necessary. Property taxes, however, represent only one component of a much broader funding problem.

When the IDEA statute was first enacted, Congress undertook to federally fund the cost of the nation's special education programs at 40%. Unfortunately, by the time that the IDEA statute made it to the appropriations stage, the heralded 40% funding level was nowhere to be seen. Although the cost of providing special education services has soared in the last decade, and while "full funding" has its supporters in Congress, the federal government still is funding only approximately 15-17% of the total cost of implementing the IDEA mandate.

In February of 2001, some months before the events of September 11 and the start of what was to be a sustained economic downturn, I testified before the House Committee on Governmental Reform on the funding issue

---

[1] School district administrators invariably will include language in the annual report to taxpayers noting that the special education budget is "mandated" by federal law. Translation: "Believe me, if the feds did not *make* us spend your hard earned money, we certainly wouldn't be spending it!"

as part of my testimony on the broader issue "Is the IDEA Statute Working As Congress intended?" I joined a number of other voices calling for a material increase in appropriations to fulfill IDEA's mandate. I did caution, however, that the answer was not simply throwing additional money to the states without accountability and oversight to ensure that additional funding is primarily utilized in a direct manner, and not used simply to fund further administrative layers.

For parents with children diagnosed with autism spectrum disorders or other disabilities that require a 24/7 "full court press," another regular source of conflict at IEP meetings is the limited and compressed *schedule* of the public school day and calendar. School districts are always trying to fulfill each child's needs during the "regular" school day. In point of fact, school districts often will tell parents of special needs children that their children's services "must" be delivered that way. Unfortunately, most parents will actually believe them!

The problem, of course, is that many disorders and disabilities are "workaholics" that do not know how to take a break, much less a weekend or holiday. This is the very essence of the term "special education." The time frame for the delivery of "special" education is something that may or may not be consistent with the time frame for the delivery of "regular" education. This is precisely why the IDEA statute and its implementing regulations expressly allow for needs-driven "extended day" (after school) and "extended school year" (summer) educational programming.

The key, as always, is establishing need. This does not mean establishing that it would be "better" or "more appropriate" for your child to have the additional services. Except in those few jurisdictions that have adopted "maximizing" statutes, need is the litmus test. Parents demonstrate need with evaluations, data, progress reports, anecdotal evidence and persuasive advocacy at the IEP meeting.

Parents trying to schedule IEP meetings will quickly notice that few, if any, school districts will offer time slots for IEP meetings that are scheduled after two or three in the afternoon.   Many school district functionaries will refuse to attend IEP meetings unless they are getting paid for their attendance. This is a good reason to try to schedule your child's meeting as early in the day as possible.

For most school district employees, the school day is over at three, the school week is considered over on Friday, and the school year is finished in June. Quite a few school district administrators regard the summer break as a hallowed, inalienable right, with the educational, administrative, and IEP process going into a form of extended hibernation. For this reason, when problems and important issues arise after the "regular" school year is over, many school district administrators will improperly attempt to persuade parents that they must wait until September to address the new issue. Unfortunately, many issues, including but not limited to behavioral reversals, cannot wait until September. Predictably, inappropriate behavioral presentments have a tendency to groove-in and become more problematic with the "benefit" of time.

Another principal cause of conflict at IEP meetings is the level of training and expertise that exists within the district. It is only natural that special education personnel want to *believe* that they have all the training and expertise they need to be able to effectively do their jobs.   Similarly, it is only natural that school district administrators want to believe that they and their staff can handle any "special needs" situation. They certainly want to be able to report as much to the school board and to the superintendent. By way of example, we all know excellent drivers who sometimes *need* to stop to ask for directions, but refuse to do so out of a false sense of pride. In the field of special education, where there is no such thing as a precise roadmap and where one must *always* be asking questions, this is a most unhelpful quality.

The fact that a person has graduated from Yale Medical School with honors does not mean that he or she is ready to perform delicate heart surgery any more than a recent Harvard Law School graduate is going to be ready and able to adequately defend a criminal defendant who has been charged with a capital defense. Similarly, the fact that someone has received a Master's degree in special education does not necessarily mean that he or she has sufficient knowledge and training about effective interventions to remediate autism or any other enigmatic disorder or disability.[2]

The following exchange took place at an IEP meeting held in the Northeast and speaks volumes as to this particular school district's lack of familiarity even with basic terminology:

CHILD'S FATHER: "With all due respect, my wife and I are not getting a confidence level that the district knows all that much about how to address our son's autism.

DISTRICT: "We appreciate your concern, but you have to understand that we have had many children in this school district who have been diagnosed with pidness.

CHILD'S FATHER: "Pidness?"

DISTRICT: "Yes. You know, PDD (NOS)."

It takes integrity and quite a bit of courage for a school district administrator to admit to parents (or to the superintendent or school board for that matter) that the school district and its personnel do *not* have the expertise and training that the child's unique needs require. Ironically, the school district that is "up front" and is able to identify and *acknowledge* its shortcomings is precisely the kind of school district that parents will want to work with!

Unfortunately, many school districts are all too willing to play fast and loose with important-sounding labels and titles such as "autism specialist," "behavior specialist" and "inclusion specialist" without first assuring that these titles are warranted and earned through training and experience.

Ostensibly, one of the principal purposes of adopting authoritative sounding job descriptions for district staff is to inspire parent confidence. In general, people are less likely to challenge visible authority figures. Parents of special needs children—especially parents who are already uncertain as to what to do with their child—are less

---

[2] In the field of autism, for example, it is not at all unusual for behavior analysts (individuals typically holding a Master's level degree) to be providing instruction and expertise to Ph.D. level "students."

likely to question or take issue with actions taken and recommendations made by someone who is identified and held out to be a genuine "specialist."

Sometimes, the school district administrator is relying in good faith upon the representations of school district personnel that they indeed possess the requisite training and expertise. To secure or continue their positions of employment, just as in the commercial world, some school district staff have been known to mischaracterize or overstate their qualifications and experience. The higher the demand is for the particular expertise, the more likely it is that someone looking to get or keep a job will "embellish" their prior experience.[3]

Unfortunately, the bona fides of these so-called "specialists" are usually not found out until it is too late. These *poseurs* are sometimes unmasked at due process during the cross-examination phase, much to the chagrin of the school district administrator who hired the person in the first place. This is what happens when school district administrators who are anxious to fill a position fail to exercise appropriate due diligence during the interview and selection process.

Parents should be wary of accepting "specialist" job descriptions at face value. When school districts trot out laudatory job classifications that hold someone out to be a "specialist," parents should not hesitate to ask the hard questions that need to be asked. What specifically is this individual's work experience? How long has this person served as the district's "autism specialist?" How many children my child's age and with my child's unique presentment has this person serviced? What is this individual's caseload and schedule? In this school district, what are the criteria for becoming an "inclusion specialist?" Who, if anyone, does this person report to within the district?"

Yet another cause of conflict at IEP meetings is ego and the perceived need for control. School district administrators and teachers feel that they are the anointed experts in special education, and they often bristle and take it personally when mere parents (who normally have no formal training as special educators) challenge or question their recommendations. This is a serious problem, since it is essential that parents ask the right questions.

---

[3] A recent study conducted by ADP found that more than 40% of Americans "pad" their resumes.

While school district administrators and teachers certainly would be expected to have a great deal of expertise in special education matters, the savvy and confident administrator knows that the parent who is living with his or her child 24 hours a day, seven days a week, has very valuable knowledge and insight.

School districts that fail to actively seek out parental input and recommendations often botch the IEP by missing the opportunity to accurately complete "present levels of performance." The school district that is not paying attention to what parents are saying often will find out at due process that at the time that the IEP was developed, the child already had mastered and met criteria with respect to many of the objectives that the school district wrote into in the IEP. It goes without saying that it is entirely inappropriate when a child is wasting precious time working on "pre-mastered" skills.

Similarly, there is a general danger that the school district will completely "miss the boat" blindly relying upon computer-generated IEP goals and objectives. In one of our due process hearings, the school district had insisted that its proposed IEP goals and objectives were entirely appropriate, and that they all had been carefully selected and tailored to meet the individual needs of the child. One of the school district's proposed IEP objectives was that "[name of child] will learn how to say 'Daddy'." While this kind of objective might have been entirely appropriate in some other child's IEP, this particular child had two, same-sex parents, but neither of them was male, and let it suffice to say that neither of them wanted to be called "Daddy." This exchange helped to provide the judge with a compelling window of insight into the supposed "individualization" of this child's IEP.

Many parents will spend what feels like every waking hour educating themselves about their child's special needs. It is an unfortunate mistake, as well as a violation of the IDEA statute, for school district administrators to ignore a parent's valuable input.

In point of fact, *the IDEA statute commands that parents are supposed to be equal members of the IEP team. The IDEA statute also mandates that IEP's are supposed to be developed by "consensus."* There are still, however, many school districts around the country that will improperly ignore parental input and present IEP's on a "take it or leave it" basis.

Finally, collective bargaining agreements with the teacher's union can give rise to conflict at IEP meetings. At least as between the school district and its personnel, collective bargaining agreements often will specify when and how often teachers and aides will take their breaks, the duties of one-on-one support aides, record keeping responsibilities, when and how teachers may be observed and assessed, the circumstances when teachers and aides can be removed from their responsibilities, and the teacher's ability to provide "discipline" when children engage in inappropriate behaviors

> *Recently, one of our client families attempted to have a well-known consultant observe their son in class for a two-hour time block of instruction. The school district insisted that the only time frame that they would consent to an observation was non-instructional time. Why? The collective bargaining agreement with the teacher's union apparently forbids "outsiders" coming in to observe/assess instruction. Aside from the obvious option of bringing an impartial hearing to break this kind of logjam, parents should first put in writing that the purpose of the observation is to assess the child's needs and learning issues, and that the focus is not on the teacher's abilities or deficits.*

There may be glaring inconsistencies, between the provisions of a collective bargaining agreement, the child's individual needs, and the requirements of the federal IDEA statute and its implementing regulations. Let it suffice to say that the IDEA statute does not provide that it is to be followed unless the teachers' union disagrees. How convenient when the school district relies upon a handicap of its own making!

As a practical matter, however, put yourself in the mindset of the school district administrator. Who would you prefer to take on—a frustrated parent or the entire teachers' union? Most school districts would prefer to take a "hit" in an individual due process hearing than face the financial and other consequences of fighting the whole teachers' union.[4]

---

[4] An even bigger problem is that the impact of collective bargaining agreements is a problem that normally operates *below* the radar screen. Parents rarely, if ever, are privy to such considerations.

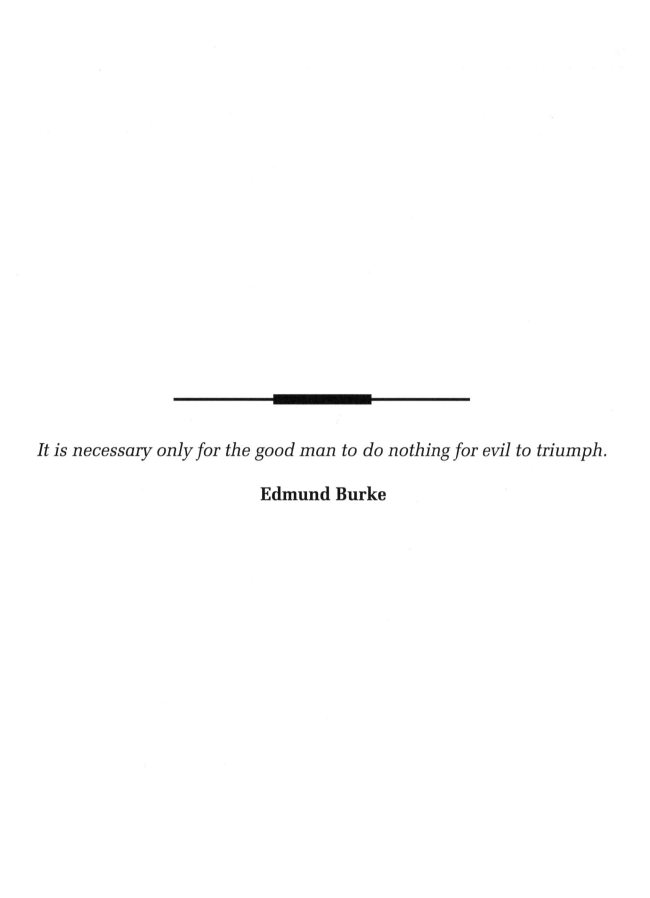

It is necessary only for the good man to do nothing for evil to triumph.

Edmund Burke

Chapter 2

Be Aware of the Language of Intimidation

Parents who have a working understanding as to why there is so much conflict at IEP meetings are less likely to be intimidated or "finessed." Along these lines, it is important for parents to be sensitive to and aware of the *language* of intimidation. This language is cultivated by certain school districts and comes in subtle and not-so-subtle variants. While certainly not exhaustive, the following statements are fairly representative of the kinds of things that school district administrators will say at IEP meetings in an effort to persuade parents to give written consent to the IEP being recommended by the school district:

➢ "We want to get services started for your child right away, but we cannot start services until you give your consent to the IEP."

➢ "I have been in special education for thirty years. Believe me, I know what I am doing."

➢ "Do you have any idea how much this school district is already spending on special education programs? What you are asking for is just not in the budget."

➢ "This is public school. We're not even going to *discuss* methodology. If you want to dictate educational methodology, perhaps you should look into a private school situation."

➤ "If we give your child what you are requesting, this will set a precedent which will open the floodgates for other families to ask for the very same thing. If we can't give it to everyone, we certainly can't give it to just your child."

➤ "Why don't we at least *start* with something and see how it goes? If a problem arises, we can always reconvene the IEP committee and decide to change the mix and quantity of services at that time."

➤ "We have had many children just like yours who have done well with the same level and type of service you are resisting. Your child really does not need any additional or different services. With all due respect, you are being more than a little neurotic. You need to relax."

➤ "We have had dozens of families in your exact situation. This may come as a surprise to you, but yours is the only family to have ever complained."

➤ "Gee, we don't know if we can allow you to take your child out of class early for specialized, oral-motor speech therapy. If your child is truant, we might be under an obligation to contact Child Protective Services. We wouldn't want you to get in any kind of trouble."

➤ "We want what is appropriate for your child, just like you do, but the services which you are seeking would be excessive and harmful to your child, and we certainly are not going to pay for your child to be harmed. Your child needs time to play just like a 'normal' child."

➤ "I don't know why you have so much concern about "behaviors. There is no need to bring in an outside behavior analyst or consultant. The classroom teacher reports that there are no behaviors that she cannot redirect or deal with and I can assure you that your child is making nice progress."

➤ "Look—your child is going to need us for many years. Do you really want to start our relationship off on the wrong foot by being so demanding?"

> ➤ "It's very insulting to our staff when you ask these kinds of questions. You really have to trust us."

> ➤ "Your child was diagnosed as having "only" a mild to moderate case of [autism, PDD, etc.] The district believes, therefore, that mild to moderate intervention is what is called for. We reserve 'intensive' services only for the most *severe* cases and luckily for you, your child is not one of them."

Faced with this kind of pressure, the inclination of many parents is to simply "go along" with pretty much whatever the school district is offering. Some parents fear that if they communicate any discontent to the school district, their children (even their typically developed children who are attending other district programs) will bear the brunt of retaliation.

Other parents feel guilty about pressing for services above and beyond what other children in the community may be receiving. Still others are too physically and emotionally drained after dealing with their child's challenges twenty-four hours a day, seven days a week. The incentive to simply "go along" can be very seductive.

Parents should be aware that some school districts, in their quest for signed and consented-to IEP's, will attempt to take undue advantage of *any* perceived vulnerability.

Even a garden variety mugger looking for an intended victim will perform a vulnerability analysis. People who live in urban areas quickly learn how to dress, act and walk so as to minimize their chances of being "selected." Unfortunately, the same kinds of behavioral principles apply to the IEP process, even though, usually, more subconscious factors will be at play. Most school district administrators are, of course, not "IEP muggers." Parents, however, need to present themselves as savvy and motivated so that if they are "selected" for anything, it is the very *best* that the district has to offer.

Just as it is a function of human behavior that the "squeaky wheel gets the grease," the same behavioral principles operate to earmark and identify those families who are *thought* to be more likely to tolerate a lesser program of educational services. For this reason, while families should, of course, make every reasonable effort to be cooperative, courteous and professional in all their dealings and communications with school districts, these same families have to be careful that they always present themselves as proactive, motivated and informed parents who, if necessary, will vigorously challenge any offer of educational services that is not appropriate. Parents who are both informed and appropriately assertive are less likely to become "IEP victims."

If the only tool you have is a hammer,
you tend to see every problem as a nail.

Abraham Maslow

Chapter 3

Why Getting the Right Evaluations
Early On Is Critical

The assessment and evaluation stage is a critical stage in the development of the Individualized Education Plan ("IEP"). In point of fact, the assessment process probably is the most critical stage, since it serves to identify the child's special needs and provides an initial template for the treatment and intervention that would appear to be necessary and appropriate. Without comprehensive and appropriate assessments and measures serving to properly identify a child's unique needs, one might as well be playing "Pin the Tail on The Donkey."

Where purely *medical* needs are concerned, we think nothing of subjecting our bodies to the most rigorous assessments and inspections. We exalt CAT scans, EKG's, colonoscopies, blood work, strep cultures, stress tests and other objective measures— measures that we rely upon to point the way to appropriate treatment regimens. We go to the best doctors. We do not hesitate to seek a second, or even a third opinion.

Inexplicably, however, school districts will often gloss over or rush through the assessment stage in assessing and "baselining" multi-faceted and complicated disorders and disabilities. Even worse, far too many parents will tolerate and accept these inadequate "rush jobs." This is a serious mistake that can result in serious consequences later on.

Note: When school district personnel perform the underlying assessments and evaluations, it is important to have an opportunity to see the actual assessment protocols and notes, to the extent they are available. In a recent case in our office, the school district's assessment personnel were very pleased to report that a child being interviewed for "kindergarten readiness" knew his home address. An examination of the interview form showed, however, that the child's response to the question "Where do you live?" was "I live on Minnie Street." In actuality, however, the child did <u>not</u> live on "Minnie Street." The child's mother realized immediately that he was simply "scripting" from a videotape. If parents do not remain vigilant as educational detectives, these kinds of situations will go unchallenged, free to perpetuate themselves in report after report. Whether for good or for bad, inertia is a powerful force.

Why do some school districts rush the assessment process? Sometimes, there is a statutory "timeline" issue that the school district administrator is trying to meet. Sometimes, there are simply too many children being evaluated at one time by too few assessment specialists. Not infrequently, the school district is uncertain, and sometimes clueless, as to what assessments and measures to employ. And sometimes, assessment personnel working for the school district are following administrative guidelines that only later will reveal themselves to be inadequate.

In assessing eligibility and the need for special education services, it is important for parents to understand that the very first step in developing an Individualized Education Plan ("IEP") is to evaluate and assess the child to determine the child's "present levels of educational performance," sometimes referred to in administrative shorthand as "PLEP" (or "PLOP" in many jurisdictions).

Once PLEP is assessed and the IEP team gets a grip on the child's individual strengths and deficits, the IEP team can then move to the development of specific goals and objectives that will properly address those very same strengths and deficits. Similarly, after the IEP team develops appropriate goals and objectives, the IEP team can then move on to the issue of selecting and recommending an appropriate placement and program. That is the sequence as it is *supposed* to happen.[5]

The stages of "building" an IEP are a lot like building a house. The assessment and evaluation stage is an early step that is akin to testing soil conditions and pouring a solid *foundation*. Getting the assessment phase done properly indisputably is the key to having any kind of a chance to get the right kinds of services and having those services start in a timely and effective fashion.

How, then, should parents ensure that the school district has secured and is relying upon the right assessments and evaluations? Many parents get good results with a prophylactic, "two track" assessment approach.

Track One: When parents contact the school district and ask for help, the very first thing that the school district is supposed to do is ask the parents to give their consent to a series of evaluations and assessments to be performed by persons employed or contracted by the *school district*. Unless patently unreasonable, consent should be given.

An entire book could be devoted to the assessment process, and when requests for consent would be considered reasonable or unreasonable. As discussed later in this book, parents should not engage in any conduct that would be considered uncooperative, unreasonable or "inequitable." On the other hand, it is not a given that parents have to blindly consent to requests that, on their face, are unreasonable.

For example, for a child living in the New York City area, with numerous assessment sites in the vicinity, it most assuredly would be unreasonable for the school district to propose that the child travel to Hartford, Connecticut for *any* testing.

---

[5] Of course, just as autism is a pervasive developmental disorder that is at *variance* with expected developmental progress, many school districts do not regularly follow the well-established order of IEP development. While not appearing in the DSM-IV, far too many school districts might be diagnosed with a malady called "IEP Development Disorder." These school districts will recklessly leapfrog *over* PLEP and the development of goals and objectives to go directly to recommending the placement and/or program. This kind of approach—one which tailors the *child* to the administrative or fiscal needs of the school district, certainly may initially save a lot of time for the IEP team, but it is an irresponsible way to "develop" an educational plan. It also is impermissible under law and statute, since it effectively *prevents* the IEP team from proposing placements and programs based on the child's unique and individual needs.

Similarly, if a school district had just completed cognitive testing in October, it probably would be unreasonable for the school district to request the same kind of testing in December.

When in doubt, however, the safest course is for parents to provide consent that is dated and in writing. The *timing* of consent is important because the school district's statutory obligation to complete assessments and convene the IEP meeting is tied in to the date that consent is given. When consent is given, there is nothing wrong with giving it <u>conditionally</u>, so long as the condition is not onerous or unreasonable. *Example*: "We consent to the speech and language testing you have requested on *condition* that a copy of the assessment and evaluation report be provided to us as soon as it is completed."

It should come as no surprise to parents that many of the assessment individuals selected by the school district either will be employed by or financially dependent upon the school district. Even if they are not performing assessments on a volume basis, most of these individuals would like to *continue* to receive assessment assignments from the school district. These individuals certainly do not wish to antagonize, much less bite the hand that is feeding them. For this reason, assessments and evaluations coming from this group may be somewhat "lukewarm," or they may lack specific recommendations (ostensibly to leave room for the school district to propose them). When assessments identify areas of need but then fail to make any recommendations to address those needs, a red flag should go up.

<u>**Track Two**</u>: If parents are at all able to afford the additional expense, parents should secure private assessments and evaluations from the best evaluators that can be located, and provide those assessments to the school district for consideration at the IEP. Parents should do this as soon as possible *without* waiting for the school district to conduct and develop its own assessments. Ideally, this is something that parents should do even *before* meeting with the school district for the very first time.

Note: Pediatric developmental specialists, speech and language pathologists, behavior analysts, and similarly situated parents are usually good sources of referral to appropriate assessment professionals.

When selecting a private provider for assessment purposes, parents should confirm in advance that the assessment report will be accompanied by specific recommendations for treatment and intervention.

After the assessment professionals communicate and explain the kinds of assessments that are going to be conducted, parents should directly ask: "If money were not an issue, what additional tests would you be recommending at this time?" Hopefully, the answer will be "none." Parents need to ask this question because some assessment professionals are unduly sensitive to the high cost of securing evaluations, and will cut off the prospect of additional expense *without* first consulting with the parents. If the assessment professional would be recommending additional testing "but for" the additional cost, the decision as to whether to pursue the additional testing should strictly be the parents' call.

The "Independent Evaluation": For those parents who have pursued only a "track one" approach, and who have received unsatisfactory and disappointing evaluations from assessment professionals selected by the school district, there still is a valuable option that can and should be exercised by parents.

When parents receive an unsatisfactory assessment from the school district, parents should request an "independent evaluation" at *district* expense.

Parents should always make or confirm this kind of request *in writing*. The school district has thirty days from the date of the request to either approve the request, or take the parent to due process over the issue i.e. the *school district* has the burden of commencing the due process proceeding. Faced with the cost of the independent evaluation and the cost of hiring a lawyer to start a due process hearing to contest a parent's request for an independent evaluation, we have found that most school districts will opt to fund the independent evaluation, either in whole or in part.

The following is an example of the kind of letter that needs to be sent when a family is interested in securing an independent evaluation at the expense of the school district:

Dear _____

My husband and I are not satisfied with the recent speech and language evaluation performed by the evaluator chosen by the district. Among other things, we do not believe that the district's evaluation sufficiently assesses our son's numerous issues regarding articulation, motor planning, and receptive/expressive deficits. With all due respect, we do not believe that the district's evaluation accurately reflects our son's unique needs.

In light of the foregoing, we are requesting that the district agree to pay for an independent evaluation of our son by [name of provider], who is a private speech and language pathologist located at _____. The anticipated cost of the evaluation is $_____.

Please advise whether the district will pay for this independent evaluation, which we consider to be essential. In the event that the district refuses to pay for the independent evaluation, or fails to advise of approval within the next 30 days, we reserve the right to secure and pay for the requested independent evaluation and if we have to go that route, we would have no choice but to look to the district to reimburse us.

Please advise. Thank you for your consideration.

Sometimes, school districts receiving a request for an independent evaluation will cheerily tell the child's parents that the request is granted, provided that the parents select the so-called "independent" provider from the list that the *school district* maintains for that purpose! This kind of response, while not necessarily illegal on its face, defeats the whole purpose of securing an "independent" evaluation.

Parents faced with this kind of conflict need not climb aboard the school district's roller coaster. When school districts attempt this tact, parents should politely, but firmly, decline and should be ready to identify the *independent* assessment provider that the parents wish to go to.

Once a parent declines to choose a so-called "independent" evaluator whose name appears on a list maintained for that purpose by the school district, it is incumbent upon the school district to allow the parent to make an independent choice, or be prepared to take the parent to due process to establish that there is no basis for *any* independent evaluation.

Whether secured at parent or district expense, parents need to get the independent evaluation report in front of the IEP committee for review and consideration as soon as possible. As soon as the report is available, parents should send it in to their child's case manager and IEP chairperson. At the very least, this is something that normally should be provided to the IEP committee *before* the IEP meeting.

If the independent assessment suggests that the child's current program and level of services are adequate, obviously nothing further need be done. On the other hand, if the independent assessment makes recommendations for additional or different services, it is essential that an IEP meeting be convened as soon as possible so that the IEP team can consider the new recommendations and take action on them, one way or the other.

Unless requested by the school district, it usually is not critical to have the independent evaluator in physical attendance at the IEP meeting. It is, however, important to communicate to the IEP team that the independent evaluator is available to answer any questions that the IEP team might have. Parents should make every effort to have the evaluator available by phone during the IEP meeting for that very purpose. If that is not possible, ask the IEP team to put any questions they might have for the evaluator in writing, and offer to get those questions answered by the evaluator within a reasonable time frame.

While evaluations are critical to the IEP process, they will need to be updated from time to time, typically on an annual basis. Children and their special needs change and evolve over time, sometimes quite dramatically. Unless needed earlier in the school year, many parents find it helpful to secure any necessary updates in the late winter or early spring, just *before* the time that the school district conducts its "annual review."

Note: Finally, evaluations are considered to be a "snapshot" of the child. The very best evaluations will recognize this limitation, and will seek to assess the child at different times across multiple settings e.g. at school, in the home, etc. This kind of multi-environment assessment approach can be very helpful when your child is diagnosed with a pervasive developmental disorder such as autism, where there is great difficulty "generalizing" learned skills across different people and environments.

Where, for example, there is compelling evidence that skills being taught in school are *not* generalizing to the home and surrounding community, this helps to provide support for "extended day" i.e. after-school support services.

It is a wise man who said that there is no greater inequality than the equal treatment of unequals.

Felix Frankfurter

Chapter 4

The Legal Relevance of Your Child's "Potential"

It is fairly universal that parents want their children to become the very best that they can become. There is an ancient and accurate adage that "mothers, no matter how old, are always looking at their children for signs of improvement." And these are the mothers of *typically* developing children!

Parents, then, are sometimes quite surprised to find out that under the IDEA (except arguably in states, like North Carolina, that have adopted "maximizing" statutes), school districts do not have any responsibility to do what is "best" for their child, because the applicable standard of care is merely one of *appropriateness*.[6]

Some courts have held that there is no duty to provide an "optimal" education that maximizes that child's potential. Other courts have employed an analogy that many school districts will invoke at IEP meetings; that the duty of the school district is to provide the equivalent of a "serviceable Chevrolet," but not a Cadillac.

---

[6] For this reason, except in states that have adopted "maximizing" statutes, parents should not expect services and programs that would serve to maximize their child's potential. Similarly, parents should *not* accept or adopt statements to that effect from the school district administrator (e.g. "Mr. Jones—we know you only want what is *best* for your daughter." When parents are confronted with this kind of statement, they need to set the record straight with a response such as "We are only here for what is appropriate; nothing more and nothing less—we understand that we are not entitled to seek an optimal education." Otherwise, the unwary parent may later be met with a record where the school district will attempt to justify a refusal to meet parental requests on the basis that the parents were seeking "optimal" or "utopian" services.

Of course, even a serviceable Chevrolet must be able to pass inspection under applicable safety and emission standards. Just like an appropriate intervention program, every car needs effective mechanisms for steering, braking and acceleration, and regularly scheduled maintenance is essential. Moreover, to the extent that the IDEA statute requires school districts to develop IEP's that are tailored to meet the individual and unique needs of each child, what may be "serviceable" and meaningful for one child may not be effective or appropriate for another. And sometimes, what is appropriate for a child also just happens to be what is best for the child.

While school districts may not be under a duty to provide "optimal" services that "maximize" a child's potential, more courts are beginning to recognize and accept the principle that a child's potential must be *considered* as an important factor in determining what kind of an education is "meaningful" for that child.[7]

If a ten-year-old child with autism, who is considered non-verbal, suddenly learns to say one word, that achievement might well warrant a celebration. On the other hand, if a higher functioning four-year-old with a pre-existing five-hundred word repertoire learns only 100 new words in one year, that achievement might be considered grossly inadequate given the many thousands of words that a child in first grade needs to become familiar with.

For the purposes of IEP development, this means that IEP goals and objectives (as well as the criteria for mastery) need to be sufficiently challenging for the child (although not patently impossible to achieve). It is a classic no-no when school districts propose low-tone goals and objectives that the child has already mastered, or is close to having mastered. This is *precisely* why it is essential that the school district properly assess a child's present levels of performance. If the school district properly assesses present levels of performance and establishes the child's baseline, this approach naturally should help protect against the situation where the school district simply "rolls over" and perpetuates the same stale goals and objectives, year after year.

While there is no general statutory duty to provide an "optimal" or utopian education that maximizes a child's potential, it must be kept in mind that the IDEA

---

[7] <u>Ridgewood Board of Education</u> v. N.E., 172 F.3d 238 (3d Cir. 1999).

statute *does* require "maximum" effort when it comes to educating children with disabilities with their non-disabled peers. A "maximizing" standard also applies to offering children with disabilities the general curriculum.

The applicable standard for purposes of Congress' mandate of "least restrictive environment" ("LRE") is that school districts must educate children with disabilities with their non-disabled peers to the "maximum extent appropriate," even if this can occur only with the assistance of supports, aids and accommodations. (34 C.F.R. Section 300.550 (b) (2))

Some school districts will *protest* that a child cannot be maintained in a less restrictive environment without providing a one-to-one aide and other supports. This is, however, precisely what Congress has mandated.

The statutory "maximizing" standards, while certainly important to promoting less restrictive settings, can be misused or abused unless the concomitant requirement of "appropriateness" also is considered. The mere existence of maximizing standards does not mean that children without prerequisite swimming skills should be thrown headlong into the deep end of the swimming pool. The thorny area of "least restrictive environment" is discussed in greater detail in Chapter 9.

*There is never a duel with the truth. The truth always wins,
and we are not afraid of it. The truth is no coward.
The truth does not need the law. The truth does not need
the forces of government. The truth is imperishable,
eternal, and immortal and needs no human agency to support it.*

Dudley Field Malone[8]

---

[8] Advancing the argument that scientific testimony supporting evolution should be admitted into evidence in the Scopes "monkey" trial — July 16, 1925.

Chapter 5

The Importance of Making and Preserving "The Record"

Guess what—school districts are making a record all the time. At least, that is what *their* attorneys tell them to do.

When school districts evaluate and assess your child, they are "making a record" in an effort to justify the types and levels of services that are going to be offered. When school districts send letters, faxes, notices, proposed IEP's or other documents, they are making a record. When school districts speak with you or your child's service providers on the telephone, they often record and "log" the date and time of the call and the substance of what was discussed. School districts are not doing this for their health—they are making a record.

School districts, by and large, have become quite adept at making and preserving the record. This is an area, however, where the efforts of beleaguered parents often will fall short. In order to level the playing field, it is essential that parents learn how to make and preserve their own record, and that parents do so religiously. In the event of a dispute, either at an IEP meeting or at due process, good record-keeping often can save the day.

A low-tech solution for parents: A parent's first and perhaps best line of defense is a spiral notebook that is available at any Staples outlet for about $.99. Every time you speak with a district representative about anything, even if it is only scheduling, you should record the date, time and substance of what was discussed or agreed upon.

If a service provider fails to show up, note the event.[9] If you are providing transportation that your school district is failing or refusing to provide, note the trip and the mileage involved. If someone gives you the name of a good service provider, note the name and telephone number. If you go in for a parent-teacher conference, record the event, and summarize what was discussed. Treat the notebook like a log, and by all means, treat the notebook as a permanent record that you never, ever throw out. Otherwise, you will have to rely on memory or, at best, hundreds of scraps of paper.[10]

The convenience and efficiency of fax machines: It is a given that parents of children with disabilities do not have a lot of extra time on their hands. For this reason, parents should make sure that they have a simple fax machine (or fax program for the computer) and/or e-mail capability so as to be able to efficiently and conveniently send and receive communications with school district personnel. The nice thing about most fax machines is that they have the capability to generate a written "confirmation" of the communication.

Today, hearing officers across the country still display a preference for letters and faxes over email. Although we are now living solidly in the information age, there still is a preference for things that are *tangible*.[11] If parents are relying upon e-mail to make a record, they should be certain to print out a hard copy of all the emails, whether sent or received, and maintain them in a separate folder for future reference. It is essential to retain the hard copies because computers are known to crash, get viruses, get stolen or have to be returned to employers.

Certified and registered mail: A word about certified or registered mail-please don't bother unless you happen to live in a state that requires communications with the school district to be by certified or registered mail. The problem with certified or registered mail (other than the hassle and expense of having to go to the post office) is

---

[9] It also is a good idea for parents to purchase a simple calendar, where parents, using their own form of "short-hand," can record their child's intervention schedule, and the extent to which interventions are actually provided.

[10] Many parents are able to get by with a single notebook for the entire year. Other parents find that it is easier for them to maintain separate notebooks for communications with school district administrators, service providers, evaluators, and teachers. Use the system that works best for your family. Choose a system that you will be able to implement and maintain.

[11] This may help to explain why in the business world, even with the advent of relatively inexpensive videoconferencing technology, commentators note that it still is important, if not critical, to have "face time."

that in order to get proof of delivery, the "little green card" has to come back signed, and even if it does, it is not always possible to recognize the signature.

"Baseline" Videotapes and Updates: Many due process cases have turned on the availability of a videotape record. In the same manner, while a picture may paint a thousand words, a videotape record may "paint" the very words you need to make your point before the IEP team.

Ideally, you will be making a brief yet compelling record of pre-treatment and post treatment conditions. At or *before* the time that treatments and interventions start, you should make a "baseline" videotape of your child left to his or her own devices, and perhaps another tape of your child's ability to meaningfully interact with peers in some purposeful and age appropriate activity.

If treatment has *already* started, and you did not make a "baseline" videotape, go through your regular family videos to see if you have any segments that would provide insight on the issue that you are trying to highlight. After treatment starts, make brief (30 minutes or less) videotape *updates* of your child in the structure of intervention, interacting with peers, and left to his or her own devices; that is, without structure.

Many parents of children diagnosed with an autism spectrum disorder are not able to look at pre-diagnosis family videotapes since, from the benefit of 20-20 hindsight, these parents will now see symptomatic and stereotypical behaviors such as toe walking, etc. that, prior to diagnosis, seemed so cute. For the same reason, many parents recoil at the thought of creating a videotape record of their child not under instructional control, because this is when many children will display stereotypical or self-stimulatory behavior.

It goes without saying that parents would prefer to record their child blowing out birthday candles or riding a two-wheeler for the first time. As painful as it may be for parents to watch or record their child manifesting *deficits*, exhibiting the deficits can prove to the satisfaction of the IEP team (or, if necessary, an impartial hearing officer) that the child *requires* the added structure of, for example, extended day intervention hours in the afternoons and on weekends (and perhaps holidays as well).

You certainly can make out a case for extended day services with other types of evidence, but it is amazing how a compelling videotape record can cut through piles of evaluations and expert reports. In one such videotape record that immediately comes to mind, a four-year-old boy diagnosed with an autism spectrum disorder is seen in his backyard repetitively opening and closing the same gate—for more than an hour. Watching that tape for 10 minutes provided all the evidence anyone would ever need to conclude that this was a child who needed additional one-to-one structure and teaching after school.

Obtaining and updating your child's educational record: At least once a year, you should make a practice of making an appointment to review and inventory your child's permanent educational record. Requesting an opportunity to inspect your child's educational record is easy. Your request should be in writing, and might look something like this:

> *Dear [Chairperson]*
>
> *At your staff's earliest convenience, I would like to make an appointment to inspect my daughter Julia's permanent educational record. In this connection, I want to be able to see Julia's raw test scores and the test protocols that were recently employed. I also want to see any documentation that specifically shows how Julia is progressing against her individual goals and objectives.*
>
> *Please advise. Thank you for your consideration.*

You have an absolute and unconditional right to inspect your child's educational record, and to bring an expert with you to do the same. This is the time when many parents find items and information they previously were not aware of. Or, they find that the contrary is true—items they believed were placed in the record are now missing. If you do find that anything is missing from your child's file and you have copies of what is missing, send them in with a cover letter explaining that you are sending in replacement documents that you found to be missing from your child's permanent educational record. Your cover letter in this regard might sound like this:

Dear [Chairperson]:

> *During my recent inspection of Julia's educational record, I noticed that there are two assessments that are missing from the file; that is, Dr. Smith's evaluation over the summer, and the cognitive testing that we recently had completed by Dr. Jones. We enclose additional copies of these reports and request that these documents again be made part of Julia's permanent educational record.*

Bring a little notebook with you when your review your child's educational record, because you may not be able to make copies of documents right then and there. Note anything that strikes you as unusual, and try to be as descriptive as possible. By way of an extreme example, one of our clients actually found a yellow "sticky" placed on an assessment report that read "Do not give this version to the parents!"[12]

Fortunately, most school districts will not engage in this kind of deceitful behavior. Do not be at all disappointed if you find that your child's educational records are entirely in order. That is what is supposed to happen!

Think of the annual review of your child's educational record the same way that you would go to the doctor for an annual checkup. Most of the time, you will be leaving with a clean bill of health.

Respond to every substantive communication: Except in those cases where you receive computer generated notices that clearly do not require a response, your antennae should go up every time that you receive a written communication from the school district. In most instances, the school district is sending you a letter so that *it* can make a record. When this happens, you need to respond appropriately and in a timely manner.

Assume for the moment that you have just received a letter from your school district accusing you of being "physically intimidating" at an IEP meeting. Further

---

[12] Some years ago, an early intervention agency inadvertently disclosed an internal memorandum which clearly was in the nature of a confidential attorney-client communication. In this memorandum, the administrator expressed as "concerns" the fact that the child's father was a savvy lawyer, and that the local early intervention agency had a "policy" of limiting Applied Behavior Analysis (ABA) service hours to no more than 10 hours per week, regardless of the child's needs. Needless to say, the existence of the internal memorandum proved to be quite damaging for the local early intervention agency. When you go to inspect your child's permanent educational record, you simply never know what you are going to find.

assume that you did nothing of the sort, and that all you did was ask pointed, but appropriate questions that the school district representatives failed or refused to answer.

One way to respond is to address the charge head on; that is, specifically refuting each and every charge:

> *"The purpose of this letter is to respond to your letter dated _____ and set the record straight.*
>
> *It is <u>not</u> true that I was 'physically intimidating' at Jack's most recent IEP meeting. Ostensibly, you are referring to the fact that <u>you</u> felt uncomfortable being asked to respond to why my son came home with bruises the other day, and why no one has written in his communication book for two weeks. While I certainly asked the direct questions that had to be asked, you failed or refused to respond to my questions. That is all that happened."*

When the school district sends you a letter stating only a few inaccurate facts, responding specifically to each statement normally is the kind of response that is called for.

Another way of responding would be to respond generally. When you respond generally, your response might read:

> *"I am in receipt of your letter dated _____. Let it suffice to say that your letter is entirely inaccurate."*

A general response might be the safest and most expedient response if you have received a letter from the school district containing numerous misstatements.

The worst possible response letter you can send is a *specific* response letter that addresses certain misstatements, but not others. The danger, of course, is that someone reading that kind of response might draw the inference (correctly or incorrectly) that any misstatements not specifically responded to are true.

Parents should be in the habit of making an appropriate record. A good record is a parent's first line of defense. When parents make a good record, it signals to the school district in no uncertain terms that this is one parent who will not accept an inappropriate educational program.

If you tell the truth, you don't have to remember anything.

Mark Twain

When a stupid man is doing something he is ashamed of,
he always declares that it is his duty.

George Bernard Shaw

Chapter 6

Making a Record When Your School District is Being Less Than Forthcoming with Direct Answers

Oscar Wilde observed that "Questions are never indiscreet—answers sometimes are." This may help to explain why in some school districts, administrators will shoot dirty looks, if not full-blown death stares, at district personnel attending IEP meetings who respond candidly when parents ask what generically can be referred to as "hard questions."[13] The following are examples of questions that have the demonstrable capacity to bring IEP discussions to a crashing halt:

➤ What, if anything, is this teacher's background and experience working with children who are in "supported inclusion?"

➤ I know that you have "an ABA program" in the school but precisely how much one-on-one ABA with data collection will my child be given on a one-to-one basis?

➤ Have any *other* children in this school district ever been approved for [the additional service or support for which you are requesting consideration]?

---

[13] It is significant to note that school districts rarely, if ever, will invite your child's classroom aide to attend the IEP meeting.

➤ Is it true that there is another child in the class who is aggressive to other children and serves as a poor model?

➤ How much time per day will my child actually have being educated with non-disabled peers? Do you have a schedule of when this will occur?

➤ Where is the *data* that the district was supposed to be collecting on my child's [behaviors, academic progress, etc.]?

➤ Is my child presenting with any behaviors that are at all interfering with his or her learning? If not, who is making the decision as to whether or not there are any behaviors that should be targeted for assessment or intervention?

➤ Why is it that my child did not meet or master any of his/her IEP goals during the most recent school year?

➤ What, if any, training will the aide have received before she starts to work with my child? Who will provide that training?

➤ Is it true that my child's 1:1 support aide is being given responsibilities involving *other* children?

➤ Who, if anyone, have you located to fill the position called for in the IEP? When do you reasonably expect the position to be filled?

➤ None of the classroom aides were in place during the month of September when school started. My child's IEP expressly called for a student to teacher ratio that required the classroom aides to be in place. When were the aides fully in place and what was the impact of this problem on the class and my child?

➤ What is the rationale for putting my child in a "time out" room? Are you aware that being put in "time out" actually is very *reinforcing* for my child because he acts inappropriately to avoid complying with demands that are being placed on him? Was any functional behavioral assessment performed to assess and determine the function of my child's behaviors?

> ➤ It seems like every week, a new substitute teacher has to come in. Just how many times has my daughter's teacher been absent this year?

> ➤ Is there anyone here who can explain the bruises that recently appeared on my son's arms?

> ➤ Our annual review meeting took place in May. Why is it that it took until the end of August, just a couple of days prior to the start of school, for us to receive the IEP?

> ➤ We consented to these evaluations back in January, when they were first requested. Why is it, then, that the evaluations did not take place until mid-March and that the reports from the evaluations were not provided to us until just today here in June, during our child's annual "review? Couldn't we have had the opportunity to review these reports at least a few days *prior* to the annual review IEP meeting?

> ➤ We would like to have an educational consultant come in to assess our child in his/her educational environment. When can our educational consultant have access to the classroom for this purpose?

> ➤ Why have all communications come to a halt in my child's "communication book?" Why are our questions going unanswered?"

In fairness, there are quite a few school districts that will answer questions like these in the candid and forthcoming way that courts require when witnesses are sworn to tell "the truth, the *whole* truth, and nothing but the truth."

Unfortunately, there are also quite a few school districts that seem incapable of providing a straight answer even with respect to plainly innocuous inquiries. What exactly are parents to do when the school district is "stonewalling" and giving parents nothing but "mumbo jumbo?"

The simple answer is that parents should be sure to make a record whenever the school district is failing or refusing to respond to legitimate inquiry. Openly tape recording the IEP meeting can be very effective.[14] Another way to make a record and put the school district on the spot is to send a follow-up letter "bulleting" the questions that were posed at the IEP meeting, and confirming in the letter your profound disappointment and frustration that the district has failed and refused to provide answers.

School district personnel are very concerned about "appearances." When a school district sees you making an effective record, it increases the likelihood that the school district will view you as a savvy and sophisticated parent to be reckoned with.

---

[14] If possible, record the IEP meeting with a small, digital recorder. The newest digital recorders are small and relatively inexpensive and can often record 10 hours at a clip. For IEP meetings that go on for hours, the alternative is switching and keeping track of numerous cassettes.

You cannot shake hands with a clenched fist.

Golda Meir

Chapter 7

Do Not Allow Your School District to Create a Record of Unreasonableness or "Inequitable Circumstances"

Most parents are completely unaware that the very same IDEA statute that confers important statutory entitlements upon children with disabilities contains a little-known provision that gives hearing officers a fair amount of discretion to sanction *parents* who engage in unreasonable or "inequitable" conduct. Where genuine inequitable conduct is present, the hearing officer has the discretion to reduce or even deny the award that otherwise would have been rendered.

While parents can shoot themselves in the foot by engaging in inequitable conduct, nowhere in the IDEA statute, however, is there any definition of the kind of unreasonable conduct that might warrant a sanction. In recent years, we have been seeing quite a few school districts trying to *manufacture* an inequitable circumstances defense. What this means is that parents really need to bend over backwards in an abundance of caution to be communicative and cooperative with school district personnel, even in the face of outrageous or seemingly inhuman treatment.

Giving notice to the school district of intent to seek reimbursement for additional or alternative programs and services: Most significantly, parents need to make sure to give sufficient *notice* to the school district whenever they intend to reject the district's programming and secure alternative programming and services at district expense.

"Notice" in this context does <u>not</u> mean that parents should quietly secure the additional service and then six months later, send the school district a bill. Essentially, if parents intend to look to the school district to reimburse them for expenses incurred by the parents in the face of an inappropriate educational program being offered by the school district, except in extreme situations involving physical safety and the like, it normally is incumbent upon parents to *raise* the reimbursement issue *before* the child is removed from the public school setting. Except in those cases where the giving of notice would amount to a futile act, the reason for the requirement of notice is to give the school district an opportunity to do the right thing.

Notice can be given at the IEP meeting: When parents make a reimbursement request at the IEP meeting itself, parents need to a) advise the IEP team that they are rejecting the placement being proposed by the school district; b) identify the concerns and problems that are standing in the way of accepting the school district's program, and c) advise the IEP team of the parents' intent to seek a placement, program or service at public expense i.e. that the parents intend to look to the school district for reimbursement.

Notice can be given by letter: In lieu of communicating the foregoing information at the IEP meeting, parents can satisfy the requirements of the statute by sending a letter to the same effect at least ten *business* days before removing their child from the public education program. This statutory requirement does not require a magical incantation or legal "mumbo jumbo." The following is an example of the kind of basic "ten day letter" that would satisfy the notice requirements of the IDEA statute:

Dear [Chairperson]

The purpose of this letter is to put the district on notice that my wife and I are rejecting the proposed IEP and the program and placement being recommended for this coming September. Among other things, the proposed IEP program does not offer our son the "special instruction" that our son needs and it is not sufficiently intensive. Additionally, we believe that the district failed to propose a setting in our son's least restrictive environment. By all appearances, the district simply proposed the one setting that it had, without regard to our son's unique and individual needs.

For September, we intend to enroll our son in a mainstream preschool setting, where he will be supported by a behaviorally trained one-to-one aide. Based on the recommendations contained in the reports we provided to the district, we also intend to start a 25 hour a week home-based ABA program to help support our son in the mainstream setting, and to promote the generalization of skills.

Please be advised that we intend to look to the school district to reimburse us for the cost of the foregoing placement, program and supports, including supervision, consultation and team meetings. We also will look to the school district to provide or fund the cost of transportation.

While it is critical for parents to be sufficiently informative, there is no corresponding punitive measure or sanction if the hearing officer concludes that it is the school district that has engaged in inequitable conduct. What this means is that the "equitable circumstances" provision in the IDEA statute stands as a potential trap—but only for **parents**.

The issue of "unreasonable" conduct transcends the mere failure by a parent to provide a "ten day notice." I once stopped a parent at an IEP meeting from throwing a stapler at a school district administrator who clearly knew exactly how to push this particular parent's "button."[15]

Whether parents are speaking with school district administrators or teachers, writing letters, considering providing consent for evaluations, or attending IEP meetings, parents should assume that their conduct may one day be assessed and examined for "inequitable circumstances" purposes.

The prospect of an "equitable circumstances" charge being leveled at you is one good reason to record IEP meetings and put virtually all communications in writing. Employing these kinds of preemptive prophylactic measures makes it very difficult for a school district to ever "manufacture" an equitable circumstances defense.

---

[15] The best advice that parents can follow in dealing with school district personnel is that no matter what happens, "stay behavioral." Ironically, this is what *school district* personnel are taught to do when dealing with frustrated or angry parents. When parents engage in behavior that could be considered hostile or otherwise inappropriate, school districts are quite adept at recording (and exaggerating) such events for posterity.

One person with a belief is equal to a force of ninety-nine who have only interests.

John Stuart Mill

Chapter 8

The IEP Meeting and Development of the IEP

Under the IDEA statute, the IEP meeting is the place where at least once a year (typically an "annual review" meeting held in the late spring), parents and school district personnel come together in an effort to reach "consensus" in the careful crafting of an Individualized Educational Plan ("IEP"). The IEP is supposed to be tailored to the individual needs of the child. In most jurisdictions, it's supposed to be "reasonably calculated" to promote *meaningful* educational progress.

I have every confidence that there are plenty of parents who are having pleasant and satisfactory IEP meetings. I am equally certain, however, that those parents are *not* the ones who are calling my office. All too often, we will hear that there is a disturbing "disconnect" between the virtual reality of what is supposed to happen at he IEP meeting, and what actually happens.

What Should Parents Wear To The IEP Meeting?

This is an easy one. The IEP meeting needs to remain focused on the individual needs of the child. For this reason, although parents need not dress up for IEP meetings, parents should dress in a respectful, neutral way that will not offend anyone or deflect or divert from the mission at hand. Leave the ripped jeans and t-shirts at home. The same goes for displays of jewelry.

On a related point, if like most people you wear or carry a cell phone, make sure to switch your phone to "vibrate" mode just before the IEP meeting starts. There are few things more unappreciated than cell phones going off in the middle of an IEP meeting. Nobody wants to sit through the opening movement of the *William Tell Overture* while the district's speech and language pathologist is trying to get through her progress report.

The Importance of "Managing" The IEP Meeting

While it is essential to come to the IEP meeting with an open mind, it also is important to try to manage the IEP process so that you are not attending the equivalent of an ill-defined "free for all."

The Importance of Managing Scheduling Issues

It is a given that school district personnel are getting paid for their attendance at IEP meetings. Accordingly, school district personnel can afford a fair amount of inefficiency. Parents, on the other hand, need to juggle work and other schedules, and they certainly do not get paid to attend IEP meetings. It often is a hardship for parents if there is no closure and the IEP meeting needs to be "continued." Accordingly, it is important to make every reasonable effort to maximize the efficiency of the IEP meeting.

When you know that your child's annual review is coming up, pick up the telephone and *suggest* dates and times that are convenient for your family, as well as other persons and professionals you might be inviting to attend the IEP meeting.[16]

Under the statute, the scheduled date of an IEP meeting is not supposed to be written in stone. Parents are entitled to reasonable accommodations so that the IEP meeting can be held at a time that is reasonably convenient for all concerned. Accordingly, if you receive a notice of an IEP meeting and the date and/or time is problematic, there is no reason to be shy in proposing another date or time. However, you should do so in writing, and here, a handwritten request will do just fine. This is the perfect opportunity to try out that new fax machine!

---

[16] Pursuant to the IDEA statute and its implementing regulations, parents are entitled to invite and bring to the IEP meeting any special education specialist or anyone else for that matter who has knowledge about the child's unique needs. This means that a parent can even bring a neighbor for "moral support."

If you or your spouse needs an early start, you might also consider requesting that your IEP meeting be scheduled as the very first meeting of the day. It is not at all unusual for school districts to accommodate working parents at 8:15 a.m., and sometimes even earlier.

Very often, parents will come to IEP meetings expecting a full discussion of outstanding issues, and will be told halfway into the meeting that "there is no time left" to discuss a certain issue, or that key personnel necessary to discuss an important issue "have to go."

Many of these kinds of situations can be avoided. First, when the IEP meeting is being scheduled, you should ask how much time is going to be allotted for the meeting. If the response is "thirty minutes" and you have half dozen problems to discuss, you know that the allotted time frame will not be sufficient, and you should ask for more time, or a different day for the IEP.

In lieu of advance scheduling, parents should ask at the *outset* of the IEP meeting how much time has been allotted for the meeting and when important players have to leave. If everyone knows at the outset when the IEP meeting is going to end, it is easier to know when to put *your* issues on the table, and you will not be seen as rude if interjecting those issues means that you have to interrupt district personnel.

Make an advance list of your anticipated questions and concerns

Whatever your questions or concerns are, memorialize them in writing, if only for your own use. Once the IEP meeting is underway, it can be difficult for parents to keep track of issues and concerns unless they are written down somewhere.

Try to provide private assessment reports in advance of the IEP

If you have any new evaluation or assessment reports, by all means disclose them to the district *before* the IEP meeting. While school districts will often dump their own evaluations *en masse* on the very day of the IEP meeting (either because of inefficiency or intentionally withholding such documentation), it is not helpful to adopt a "tit for tat" approach, because delay undoubtedly will ensue, and delay in the IEP process rarely, if ever, is helpful to children with disabilities. Moreover, if litigation results, you build a much better record for yourself if the evidence shows that *you* were at all times forthcoming with information, while the district was not.[17]

Parents Should Request the *District's* Evaluations and Assessments Well In *Advance* of the IEP Meeting

Many parents are all-too-familiar with the following scenario: In or about January, the school district will request the parents' consent for a series of evaluations and assessments. Consent is given, the evaluations and assessments take place in February and March, and that is the last time the parents hear a peep about the new evaluations until May or June, during the "annual review."

At the beginning of the annual review IEP meeting, the school district administrator starts handing out all of the assessment reports, apologizing for the obvious delay. Let it suffice to say that parents are already overwhelmed by the IEP process and do not need to be in the position of having to deal with surprises— especially surprises that may operate to delay, if not effectively short-circuit, a parent's right to request an "independent evaluation."

When consent for the evaluation/assessment is sought, consent can be given conditioned upon the district's obligation to provide the parent with the resulting evaluation report within a reasonable time after the assessment is completed. For example, consent can be provided as follows: "We consent to the district's request to conduct cognitive testing on our son on the express condition that the district provides us with a copy of the test results within 30 days of the testing."

There is nothing magical about the number 30. Perhaps the assessment report can be made available immediately after the testing. Or, perhaps the district will ask for a 45-day time frame to produce the report. The important thing is that parents should press to have the district's assessment reports sufficiently in *advance* of the IEP meeting so that, at the very least, parents can have a meaningful opportunity to consider the import of the school district's reports, and whether it is advisable to seek the input of

---

[17] On the other hand, if the school district is in the process of completing evaluations, and you have received an assessment on the same subject matter, you might consider *deferring* production of your private report just to make sure that the district evaluation is "fresh" and not in any way tailored to rebut or respond to your private evaluation.

other professionals. If it is necessary to secure an independent assessment, you want to do this quickly and in sufficient time so that it does not unduly delay the IEP process.

Regardless of whether parents condition consent to evaluations on the early production of assessment reports, parents should document a request *prior* to the IEP meeting for the advance disclosure of any and all reports and assessments that the IEP team intends to consider.

Getting your issues and questions on the table

I know that some school districts will deeply resent what I am about to say, but the fact is that quite a few school districts will conduct a subtle, unduly controlling "filibuster" of sorts during the IEP meeting. This is the IEP meeting where the school district administrator orchestrates things so that school district personnel seem to do all the talking. The parent waits and waits, but never seems to get an opportunity to say anything.

These school districts that orchestrate those kinds of IEP's know all too well that when the district's agenda and "rollercoaster" stops, that is precisely when parents are more likely to start asking for things that the school district will then resist. Too many parents report that the IEP meeting is concluding and they are being hustled out the schoolhouse door to make way for the "next family" before the school district even addresses, much less responds to their specific issues.

When a school district thinks that a parent is about to ask for something significant, this often is the time that the school district decides that it is going to need to have seemingly endless IEP meetings to "revise IEP goals and objectives." Or, new and different evaluations and/or observations will be requested. When this occurs, the school district's objective is simple—delay.

In order to break this kind of logjam and force the issue, sometimes it can be helpful to provide the school district with a proposed agenda, or a document along the lines of "Items We Are Asking the School District to Consider." This is something tangible that parents can leave the school district with, particularly if the IEP meeting ends while discussions are still ongoing. The following is an example of this kind of document:

ITEMS WE ARE ASKING THE SCHOOL DISTRICT TO CONSIDER

✔ *Functional Behavioral Assessment (and behavior plan)*

✔ *Regular, ongoing support of experienced behavior analyst*

✔ *Regular team meetings*

✔ *Communication book between home and school*

✔ *Extended day programming to eliminate interfering behaviors and promote generalization*

✔ *Extended school year (Summer) programming to forestall anticipated regression*

✔ *Aide for camp to work on social and communication goals*

✔ *Transition plan for next school year*[18]

Sending a follow-up letter identifying concerns and confirming requests made at the IEP

If the school district administrator abruptly announces that the IEP meeting needs to end in five minutes and insufficient time has been set aside to address parental concerns or consider the parents' requests, parents can write a follow-up letter to the school district with their concerns and requests. Parents can send a follow-up letter even if they did not provide the school district with anything at the IEP meeting itself:

Dear [Chairperson]

We have had an opportunity to review the IEP that was provided to us at our son's IEP meeting last week. Based on our review [and input from other professionals], there are significant [insurmountable] problems with the district's proposed IEP that we were not able to discuss, given the time constraints that the district imposed. By way of example [select any that apply]:

---

[18] Of course, these items are by way of example only. Moreover, before parents "drop" this kind of document on their school district, they should first listen very carefully to what the school district has to offer.

➢ *We were not treated as equal members of the IEP team. From our perspective, the placement and program was entirely predetermined in advance*

➢ *The requests that we made for additional services are not even referred to in the IEP*

➢ *The IEP provides insufficient levels of service for our son's individual needs.*

➢ *The proposed goals and objectives are insufficiently challenging*

➢ *[Many of] the proposed goals and objectives are ambiguous*

➢ *The IEP fails to appropriately address our son's interfering behaviors*

➢ *The IEP fails to appropriately consider "least restrictive environment"*

➢ *The goals and objectives are not objectively measurable*

➢ *The criteria for mastery are not objectively measurable*

➢ *The placement that is being proposed is not appropriate*

➢ *The related services [or the levels of related services] are inadequate and inappropriate*

➢ *The IEP generally fails to offer our son "special instruction"*

➢ *The IEP arbitrarily cuts off existing IEP services*

➢ *The IEP proposes major overnight changes without an appropriate transition plan*

➢ *The IEP fails to account for our son's need for consistency and continuity*

➢ *The IEP fails to make provision for appropriate consultation/supervision*

➢ *The IEP fails to make provision for "team meetings"*

➢ *There are insufficient waypoints to assess our son's progress*

➢ *The IEP fails to propose adequate supports and accommodations that are necessary to support our son in his least restrictive environment*

➢ *The district failed to consider the "full continuum" and had no options to present other than the one placement our son is being "shoehorned" into*

➤ *The IEP is not even completely filled out*

➤ *We were given inadequate notice of the IEP*

➤ *The district did not allow sufficient time for an appropriate IEP to take place*

In view of the time constraints imposed by the district, we were not able to meaningfully address, much less discuss our request that the school district provide our son with extended day services and programming including 15 hours per week of ABA support, 3 hours per week of additional speech and language therapy, and 2 hours per week of consultation time from a board certified behavior consultant.

Sincerely,

Choosing the Correct Classification Category

Prior to the time that a child turns five years old, the child's eligibility classification typically is fairly generic (e.g. "preschooler with a disability"). Before the age of five, there is no federal statutory obligation to select a more specific disability. Ostensibly, the theory is that a child's special needs may change or may not fully or accurately unfold until the child turns five, and that therefore, children should not be saddled at an earlier age with a disability classification that may turn out to be inaccurate or even unnecessary. At least that's the theory.

Note: For children who are diagnosed with an autism spectrum disorder— a diagnosis that can now be made with relative accuracy well before the child's second birthday, the lack of a specific "autism" disability classification before the age of five can lull unsuspecting parents into a false sense of security. Even today, parents of preschoolers with autism who are presenting as being nonverbal, or who display stereotypical behaviors will be told by uninformed pediatricians to "Just give it time." Unfortunately, for these children, time without appropriate intervention is the enemy.

When a child is about to turn five years old, the IEP team must consider IEP eligibility based on more specific administrative classifications. This time frame is a critical juncture that requires careful navigation. The general rule of thumb is that parents should press for the most *specific* and accurate classification that is available at that time. Where there are *multiple* (comorbid) diagnoses, parents should generally select the classification that is consistent with the predominant disability.[19]

Sometimes, the appropriate classification is obvious enough. Where an otherwise typically developing child has suffered a traumatic brain injury during the course of an automobile accident, Traumatic Brain Injury (TBI) is specifically available as an eligibility classification.

Parents of children diagnosed with an autism spectrum disorder (e.g. ASD, PDD (NOS), Asperger's Syndrome, etc.), on the other hand, are often quite surprised to learn that "autism" is the *only* autism-related administrative classification that they can select for IEP purposes.

Some parents fear that their child will be stigmatized by an "autism" classification. In actuality, the far greater fear, particularly at the onset of intervention, is that a different classification category (e.g. speech impaired, other health impaired, etc.), may mean that the child will not be offered the very services and interventions that are required to promote remediation. This is especially true in states like New York, where there are special and additional *protections* for children classified as having "autism."[20] If your child has an autism spectrum disorder, you will want to take advantage of these special protections.

---

[19] This analysis can be difficult in the situation where one or more comorbid disabilities *change* over time. For example, while it is quite unusual, we have had the situation where there was an initial classification of "autism," and thereafter, it was discovered that the child also had severe Dyslexia. Over time, with significant remediation of the child's autism presentment, Dyslexia ultimately became the child's predominant issue and for that reason, the child's parents called an IEP meeting for the purpose of changing the child's eligibility classification to the more specific learning disability (Dyslexia).

[20] In New York, having an autism classification means enhanced speech and language entitlements, as well as "parent training." Children should not miss out on helpful and needed services because their parents chose a less than accurate classification, or because the school district administrator promoted one. Today, there are many children with autism succeeding meaningfully in public school settings. Some even go on to college and beyond. Having a disability does not carry the same kind of stigma that it would have had just 10 years ago. Today, the anticipated stigma of a specific classification probably is about the least compelling consideration.

The issue of classification can be confusing when a parent is considering classification under a *specific* learning disability, such as Dyslexia, where there also is an option to select classification under the generic and *non-specific* "other health impaired" (OHI).

At first blush, OHI can be a seductive choice for parents since, on its face, it sounds so generic and it does little to highlight the child's actual deficits. However, parents who choose that kind of classification may find that their child's services are equally generic.

Sometimes, having the *specific* learning disability classification, as in the case of a child diagnosed with Dyslexia, is the only way to justify school district support for Orton-Gillingham, Wilson Method, or other special instruction needed by the child to meaningfully remediate the Dyslexia.

In point of fact, today there are quite a few colleges and universities that will provide supports and accommodations for children who have been classified with a *specific* learning disorder or disability. Some colleges and universities, however, will *resist* extending supports and accommodations to the child who had been diagnosed with a more generic classification i.e. "other health impaired."[21] The underlying message is clear enough—do not delay to go for the most accurate and specific eligibility classification that is available.

Present Information *Visually* Whenever Possible

There is a reason why videotapes have the power to speak volumes. It is important to keep in mind that, in general, most people are visual learners. This is especially true today in our world of compressed information and decreased attention spans. We live in a world of sound bites and digital imagery. A five minute videotape often can tell a story better and more persuasively than a thirty-page brief.

---

[21] For college planning purposes, parents also should be aware that it is important to get "extra time" and other testing accommodations written into the IEP long <u>before</u> the time frame when children are taking the SAT. If there are longstanding IEP (or Section 504) testing accommodations, it is virtually automatic that the child will be eligible for the same kind of testing accommodations on the SAT. If, however, testing accommodations are not secured until just before the SAT time frame, application for special accommodations on the SAT must be made, and these accommodations are not automatically granted.

Summary graphs and other *visual* presentations of information will almost always trump individual facts and data that require deductions to be made and inferences to be drawn. Why present a series of disparate "dots" that will need to be "connected" when you can tell a story by presenting the whole picture? Once again, it is not so much what you say, but *how* you say it.

A chronology is a good tool, but a visual "timeline" can be even more effective, leaving an IEP team with a most compelling image. Consider the following timeline[22] for its potential impact on an IEP team considering a parent's request to *reinstitute* a home-based ABA program that had been discontinued by the IEP team:

---

[22] Source: TimeMap 3 - Used by permission of Casesoft (www.casesoft.com)

JASON'S TIMELINE

May 24, 2004

At Jason's "annual review" IEP meeting to develop an IEP for the 2004-2005 school year, the District recommends, based on Jason's excellent progress, that Jason's 1:1 support aide be discontinued as of September, 2004, when Jason will be entering mainstream kindergarten. The District also recommends that as of September, 2004, all of Jason's extended day services be discontinued. The District refuses Jason's parents' request to continue his aide and additional support services pending a further review in the Fall. The District also refuses Jason's parents' request for a "transition plan."

Sep 6, 2004

Jason starts kindergarten in the 2004-2005 school year without a support aide, and without any of the additional extended day support services that he had in the 2003-2004 school year.

Sep 10, 2004

Jason pulls the ponytail of girl sitting in front of him in class and is given a half-hour "time out."

Sep 19, 2004

Jason has now accumulated a half-dozen "time outs" and his teacher is reporting frustration that the frequency and severity of his behaviors is on the rise, and that the "time outs" do not seem to be effective. In addition, there are now new and different "behaviors" to contend with.

Sep 26, 2004

At parents' request and expense, a board certified behavior analyst observes Jason in his classroom and concludes that district staff *inadvertently* are reinforcing Jason's inappropriate behaviors, and that the frequency of inappropriate behaviors is even higher than reported by the district.

Oct 5, 2004

Jason is suspended.

Oct 16, 2004

Jason has now been suspended three times.

Apr 2004   Jul 2004

Lobby In Advance for Supporters Who Might Help You Build a "Consensus" at the IEP In Favor of Your Child

IEP decision-making is required to be by "consensus." Typically, however, there is no voting at IEP meetings. Usually, the so-called "consensus" is the district administrator communicating a recommendation that the other school district personnel either bless or fail to challenge.

At an appropriate juncture in the IEP meeting, the district administrator might say something like "I think that we should send Joey to the district's multiple-handicap classroom. What do you think?" If you look around the table and see the heads of all the other district functionaries bobbing up and down, you probably have just witnessed a form of "consensus" even if you are in complete disagreement with the recommendation.

While IEP decision-making can appear to be predetermined (and often is), parents should not underestimate their ability to affect the outcome of the IEP meeting by buttonholing, if not lobbying, school district personnel in advance of the IEP.

Parents should make an effort to speak with their child's classroom aide, teacher and related service providers. Is your child receiving sufficient one-to-one instruction? What kinds of behaviors is the aide (or teacher) contending with? What is standing between your child and a less restrictive setting? Would the aide (or teacher) support a request for additional or different educational programming? What are your child's greatest achievements and strengths? What are your child's greatest deficits? What kinds of records are being maintained to track your child's progress?

Allies enlisted from within the ranks of the school district can be very persuasive advocates who can change the course of an IEP meeting in a most positive way for your child. If the school district's own speech and language pathologist openly advocates at the IEP meeting for additional service hours for your child, it is more difficult for the district's administrator to say "no."

Regardless of the school district's position, it is extremely helpful for parents to try to speak with school district personnel in advance of the IEP meeting. Even if you are unable to garner any support for a position you hope to advance at the IEP meeting, at the very least you will be better apprised as to what to expect.

Consider and Look At Anything Potentially
Within the Realm of Reasonableness

It is important for each side to come to the IEP meeting with an open mind. This is not to say that parents and school districts will come to the meeting with an entirely "blank slate." Each of us arrives at the IEP meeting with our own baggage of assumptions and preconceptions. It is a given, therefore, that some strong beliefs and opinions may have formed even before the IEP meeting starts. Neither side, however, should predetermine their ultimate position.

In considering the full continuum, it is important, indeed required, for school districts to consider alternative placements and programming that parents put on the table for consideration. By the same token, it is very important for *parents* to consider placements that the school district asks the parents to consider.

Regardless of what reports you may already have received, make an appointment to actually *see* and assess the placements being considered by the school district. You might wish to engage an educational consultant, an existing teacher or therapist, or some other professional to accompany you to conduct the observation. Absent extraordinary circumstances, it is essential to go through this process *before* making any decision to engage in self-help.

Note: When parents go to see placements that are being proposed by the school district, it is important for them to stay as objective and "behavioral" as possible in describing what they specifically observed. It is not at all effective or helpful when parents take notes such as "Teaching sucks" or "Teacher cannot teach to save her life."

It is much more effective when parents act as an objective observer (e.g. "There were 28 children in the class but only one aide. Only approximately five children were observed to display any expressive language. Three children were engaging in self-stimulatory behaviors without redirection during our entire visit. One child cried and tantrummed for about 20 minutes without redirection. He ultimately was removed from the classroom").

Do Not Allow Yourself to Be Pigeonholed By Your
School District into Making A "Sophie's Choice"

Some school districts will attempt to convince you that there is some maximum or other arbitrary number of hours that they may allocate to your child. Once you buy into the "rations" or "pizza pie" concept of a "maximum" or "limited" number of service hours, the next step is to ask you—the parent—to make the determination as to how to *allocate* those hours.

Making parents decide the *allocation* of "rations" helps to legitimize the very system of arbitrarily rationing a maximum number of service hours. After all, psychologically, it is harder to complain about a choice that you made.[23]

In practice, school districts that implement a rations-type approach will tell the parent at the IEP meeting that the child may have a total of 25-30 service hours per week, and that it is up to the *parent* as to how to allocate those hours. A parent may be able to secure an extra hour of speech therapy, but that hour might then have to "come out of" some other service the child may also need. In essence, this kind of approach requires parents to "cannibalize" their children's existing service hours. This is a "Sophie's Choice" that parents should not be put in the position of making. If your child needs additional service hours (e.g. for "team meetings"), these additional service hours should, in fact, be "in addition to" your child's existing program. They should not have to "come out of" any existing service hours.

Tell your district that you are puzzled by its allocation approach because you had heard that under the IDEA statute, your child would receive an individualized program. If your school district persists with this kind of approach, make sure that you create a record in some way to show that you disagree with the district's allocation approach and that there was no genuine "choice" on your part. Ask for a note to that effect to go in the "parent's concerns" section of the IEP. In the alternative, fax your own note to the district and ask that it be placed in your child's permanent educational record.

---

[23] This is precisely how some school districts attempt to intimidate parents into believing that since they "chose" the child's evaluator, there is no opportunity to challenge the evaluation or request an "independent evaluation." These school district will present parents with a list of "approved" assessment professionals to "select" from.

In the end, you need to be able to counter any claim by the school district that the allocation of service hours was *your* idea. If your child is going to be subject to an allocation approach, let it be *imposed* on your child.

When to Punt—How to Accept Services "Without Prejudice"

Assume that certain professionals are telling you that your child needs at least five hours of speech and language therapy per week delivered on a one-to-one basis, and that two of those hours should be devoted to oral-motor therapy because of your child's motor planning issues.

Now further assume that when you go to your child's IEP meeting, the district advises that the most it can offer is two hours per week of speech and language therapy, but that there is nobody in the district with oral-motor expertise and training.

Faced with this dilemma, some parents might reject the district's offer, send the district a "ten day notice", and file for due process to seek to obtain reimbursement for the full five hours per week of speech and language therapy. However, in most cases, the remedy does not have to be an "all or nothing" proposition. Parents often can mitigate the situation and their financial exposure.

Why ever cut your nose to spite your face? Is there a problem with <u>all</u> the educational components that are being offered by the district (e.g. lack of quality, training, consistency, etc.)? Is the school district insisting that services be an "all or nothing" proposition?[24] If not, parents should try to accept the acceptable and appropriate educational components being offered by the school district on a "without prejudice" basis.

By accepting, "without prejudice", those services that are appropriate, your child can access a certain level of services (at school district expense) while, at the same time, communicating to the school district that the overall program of services it is offering is not adequate and appropriate.

---

[24] This kind of situation sometime occurs when parents are rejecting a more restrictive school placement in favor of a less restrictive setting. In that situation, some school districts will take the position that they will *only* provide related services (speech, occupational therapy, etc.) in the school district's (more restrictive) setting. When the school district *prevents* the parent from accessing services except in conjunction with other programming that is considered objectionable, parents are left with little choice but to send out a "ten day notice" or make the decision to assume the entire expense of the alternative educational program.

There is little, if any, downside to accepting services on a "without prejudice" basis. You are making and preserving a record and the subtle hint at a possible due process hearing down the road may actually free up additional service hours that otherwise would never have been offered.

How to Effectively Challenge the District's Recommendations

Parents understandably are anxious to register any complaints about the adequacy of educational programming. Parents typically harbor the concern that teaching staff will become unduly defensive and directly or indirectly "take it out" on the child (or one of their other children).

Parents also question whether their requests or challenges will ever really translate into appropriate corrective action. To be certain, no parents pine to be branded as town pariahs or "the parents from hell."[25] Just how, then, should parents communicate requests to take corrective or remedial action? As is usually the case, it is not so much what you say, but rather *how* you say it.

To the extent possible, parents should make every reasonable effort to neutralize the theme that "this is what parents want." When educational requests and challenges are coming from (mere) parents, it is all too easy for school districts to *dismiss* or give short shrift to those requests on the basis of the school district's perception that its staff has superior knowledge and training, and the often erroneous presumption that parents really don't know that much about their own children's educational needs. It is much harder, however, to dismiss or explain away recommendations that are coming from experienced *professionals* who have special knowledge concerning the child's unique needs.

To the extent possible, parents should make every reasonable effort to respect and work within the school district's established "chain of command." Most school districts follow generally accepted protocols for reporting, communication and

---

[25] On the other hand, I have seen the all-too-frequent phenomenon of normally timid and quiet parents who, over time, have been *turned into* "parents from hell" by school districts that failed and refused to listen to those parents and treated them with disdain and disrespect. To that extent, subject to being misquoted out of context, I would have to say that some of our very best clients, pressed to the wall by their respective school districts, became card-carrying members of "parents from hell."

responsibility. Very often, there also are collective bargaining agreements that impact the existing management protocols.

In most school districts, for example, classroom aides will report to the classroom teacher, and the classroom teacher will then report to a head teacher or administrator. For this reason, many teachers and school district administrators will react negatively, to say the least, when they learn that a parent has come into the classroom to *directly* confront the child's classroom aide (or teacher, for that matter) with criticism or recommendations.

The protocol for parent communication need to be established in advance, when your child's IEP is being developed. At your child's IEP meeting, you should ask your district to propose protocols to be followed if you have concerns from time to time that need to be addressed, but are not serious enough to warrant a full-blown IEP meeting. Perhaps a "communication book" is all that will be needed. If, however, the district fails to propose any protocols for communication, you hardly can be blameworthy if you then have to cross any of the established lines of authority to get your point across.

If, despite your best efforts, effective communication continues to be a problem, request an IEP meeting in writing and be certain to invite anyone who is part of the problem.

<u>Parents should take the time to recognize meaningful progress and compliment school district staff for genuine and visible achievements</u>. No parent need pay a compliment where it is unwarranted, or where it would constitute shameless pandering or bootlicking. If you ever need to challenge the school district's program, bear in mind that the school district may very well produce the Christmas card in which you lavished love and praise on everyone involved with your child's program because you got caught up in the holiday spirit.

On the other hand, you should not hesitate to pay compliments where they are warranted. When a school district administrator receives a letter or telephone call from a parent, you want to neutralize the "uh oh" factor (the immediate assumption by the school district that a complaint is about to be communicated). You also want to encourage effective teaching and essentially *any* behaviors by the school district that are helpful in promoting your child's educational progress.

Paying compliments when they are genuine and warranted gives you "credit in the bank," so that when you do communicate a complaint, it is more likely to be treated seriously.

Compel the IEP team to confront your child's deficits. While parents should take the time to recognize and appreciate educational progress and positive behavior on the part of school district personnel, parents should be cognizant of a disturbing phenomenon that sometimes will occur in the context of the IEP meeting.

The situation is one of imbalance, where virtually all of the school district reports and assessments speak glowingly of the child's progress and strengths, with almost no discussion of any deficits, problem areas, or IEP goals that were difficult to address or achieve.[26]

If you go to the dentist with a painful cavity, you don't want to hear the dentist going on and on about all of the teeth that are in good shape. It goes without saying that you must first *spot* problem areas before you can address them. This is not an issue of being negative. It is an issue of candidly confronting the positive and the negative. How then, should parents deal with the school district that is in denial?

The independent evaluation is one tool that parents have to combat this problem. If your school district is not confronting your child's deficits, by all means pay for an independent evaluation yourself if you can afford to do so. If your school district is in denial, the last thing you want to do is argue for two or three months over who will be paying for the independent evaluation.

A *brief* videotape presentation of your child left to his or her own devices can be very effective. Parents also can "audit" individual goals and objectives not referred to in the district's progress reports by asking the classroom teacher point blank at the IEP meeting: "Can he/she do this consistently?" Where the answer is a simple "yes," parents should not be shy to request supporting data. Where the answer is "no," parents should take notes of the teacher's responses and then send the school district a follow up letter confirming what may well be a *pattern* of not mastering IEP goals and

---

[26] Typically, these kind of assessments start with a *bon mot* such as "Johnny is a very handsome boy" and end with "Johnny is a pleasure to have in my classroom and I look forward to seeing him again next year."

objectives. The key is to "get behind" conclusory, one-sided progress reports to give them balance and perspective.

Parents should make every effort to "protect the record." The worst kind of confrontation at an impartial hearing is one that pits the *credibility* of a school district administrator against the credibility of a parent. The garden variety "he said, she said" evidence typically presents that kind of uncomfortable swearing contest. There is no reason for parents to put themselves into that kind of position.

To the extent possible, tape record every IEP meeting and certainly confirm in writing important undertakings made by the district even if the district does not do so. In that regard, remember that your fax machine is your new best friend. Much like online banking, it is a "passkey" that can get you into the administration building after hours, on weekends, and even during holidays.[27]

Pick Your Battles Carefully: Parents should not shrink from raising and clearly communicating any and all issues that are *genuinely* important to the delivery of an appropriate education. It is a given that behavioral, academic, staffing and other problems will arise from time to time, without regard to the convenience of parents and school administrators. After all, many disabilities (e.g. autism spectrum disorders) are classic "workaholics" that do not take a break, much less a vacation.

It also is to be expected that some children will be more "high maintenance" than others—sometimes a lot more. This is the nature of special needs children. No parent relishes ever having to call his or her school district with "problems." In point of fact, parents dread having to make these kinds of telephone calls about as much as school district administrators dread receiving them.

When, however, parents are inundated with a host of unresolved problems and feel as though they have come "under siege," it is easy to lose perspective. When smaller issues and non-issues have become intertwined with the overarching, critical issues, it is important for parents to understand that they often will lose power and

---

[27] The nice thing about fax machines is that they typically will provide a written *confirmation* establishing the date and time of transmittal, and whether the transmittal "went through." The other nice thing about faxes is that working parents have the opportunity to send them in the evening, when they are engaged in their "other job." Today, faxes (and e-mails) are generally accepted by hearing officers and judges as competent and admissible documentary evidence.

credibility with the school district when they call the school district on the carpet for *every* conceivable issue and glitch. One school district administrator has referred to this problem as one where the parent "never met an issue he/she didn't like."

The proper approach generally is a matter of exercising old-fashioned common sense and taking a step back to gain a broader perspective. It also can be a matter of how and when problems are presented. You can and certainly should provide an extensive and comprehensive "punch list" of issues and problems at an annual review type of IEP meeting. You also can request an interim IEP meeting to address a change of providers, the need to change goals and objectives, a major behavioral reversal, or some other specific problem.

Generally, in between IEP meetings, a more *focused* approach is called for. When you pick up the telephone to call the school, you want the responsible school administrator to have the reaction "Boy, this must be important." You want to maximize the odds of receiving a return call quickly. You don't ever want to desensitize the school district to by "crying wolf" on every issue or overstating the situation.[28] In short, pick your battles wisely.

On the flip side, however, is a caveat. Parents should resist efforts by some school districts that will seek to impose an arbitrary "prioritization" of important issues, on the grounds that the school district has *only so much time in the day* to deal with what it already is dealing with between 8:30 a.m. and 2:30 p.m. By way of example, assume that a six-year-old child with an autism spectrum disorder has not learned appropriate toileting skills and also presents with "interfering behaviors." It would be inappropriate for the school district to resist developing and implementing a toileting program in the child's IEP on the grounds that it is somehow *more important* to address the interfering behaviors *first*.

---

[28] On the other hand, some parents report the unfortunate situation of encountering "burned out" school district administrators and teachers who will *always* react negatively and inappropriately no matter who is calling, and regardless of the issue. To the extent that it "takes a village" to properly educate even a typically developed child, it takes only one misguided administrator to wreak havoc upon a disabled child's education program. This unfortunate situation highlights the classic problem of a chain only being as strong as its weakest link. Thankfully, most school district administrators are consummate professionals who want to do their very best, and who have not lost their zeal or compassion.

The answer, of course, is that the school district should properly address *both* of these important issues at the very same time. With the availability of "extended day" services—services that may be delivered after school, in the early evening, and even during weekends and holidays—school districts need not wring their hands about the self-created limitation of "only so much time in the day."

The choice is fairly stark; spend and "invest" the time now, or spend much more time (and money) chasing the problem later, after it has had the time to grow and become an even bigger, if not insurmountable, problem. Parents often have to spend considerable time convincing school district administrators to take the "long view," rather than focus unduly on this year's budget.

Parents need not wait for the annual review IEP meeting, typically held in the late spring, to address the problems and issues that inevitably come up during the school year, or even during the summer. Parents can and should request an interim IEP meeting whenever there is a need to do so. The following is an example of a request for an interim IEP meeting:

Dear [Chairperson]

I am requesting that you schedule an IEP meeting for my son _____ as soon as possible. The purpose of the meeting would be to discuss the adequacy of his current program and placement, and whether any of his educational components need to be changed in light of the enclosed evaluation report from Dr. _____.

Dr. _____is prepared to attend the IEP meeting to answer any questions that you may have. She also is prepared to attend via telephone. It would be best for my schedule and Dr. ____'s schedule if the IEP meeting was scheduled the first thing in the morning (8 or 9 a.m.). Unless you think that a longer time frame would be more appropriate, I am anticipating that we may need two or three hours to fully discuss the issues raised by Dr. ____'s report.

In addition to the purely educational/academic issues, I also want to discuss how the district can remedy my son's bus ride to school. The school is only 15-20 minutes away by car and yet, I am receiving reports that it is taking the bus over an hour to get to school and that my son is half-asleep when he gets off the bus. I sincerely hope that you will be able to iron out this problem with the bus company even before the meeting.

Please propose a few dates and times for the IEP and I will get right back to you. It will expedite matters if you leave a message on my home answering machine at _____ or send an email to me at_____.

Thank you for your consideration.

Sincerely,

Parents Need To Stay "Behavioral": It is almost a given that well-intentioned school district personnel will sometimes say inflammatory or ignorant things at IEP meetings that would make any parent's blood boil. This is the time when it is essential to stay calm, collected and "behavioral," in very much the same way that you might deal with a child presenting with inappropriate behaviors.

Faced with such a situation, parents will have the urge to cry out "This person is a blithering idiot and I don't want him/her having anything to do with the education of my child!" Parents must transcend the natural urge to go on the offensive and find a way to defuse the situation in a helpful, neutral and non-stigmatizing way. Once again, it's not so much what you say, as how you say it.

Sometimes, the statement made by the school district functionary at the IEP meeting will be so ludicrous that the parent does not need to say anything in response. Several years ago, a school psychologist in attendance at the IEP of a child with autism proudly described how the child was destined to be an art critic: "I was watching Peter in class the other day and saw that he was looking at this modern art painting of concentric circles. Peter was tilting his head, looking at the painting for what had to be more than an hour. I don't know why people say that Peter is so distractible. Peter was focused on that painting like a laser beam and I was amazed at the level of detail he must have been able to appreciate. I'll bet that one day, Peter becomes an art critic."

As it turned out, it was entirely unnecessary for the child's parent to say a word in response. By the exchange of glances, it was apparent that all of the other school district personnel in attendance at this child's IEP meeting were familiar enough with autism stereotypy to know that Peter's unusual focus on concentric circles was a negative, and not a positive. The school psychologist's revelation embarrassed the classroom teacher, who clearly should have had the student engaged in some purposeful and appropriate activity. Chagrined, it was the *teacher* who suggested having a behavioral consultant come into the classroom to do a Functional Behavioral Assessment.

IEP meetings should encourage communication, brainstorming, and the free flow of ideas. Some ideas may represent sheer genius. Other ideas may be fit only for the wastebasket. Expect to have to separate the wheat from the chaff. It's all part of the process.

The Pros and Cons of Bringing Counsel with You to the IEP: Unless English is a client's second language, it always is a dilemma when clients ask us to attend an IEP meeting. While the presence and support of counsel tends to make most clients more comfortable, aside from the obvious cost considerations, there actually are a number of reasons why it might actually be better if attorneys are *not* in attendance at the IEP meeting.

In the first instance, while the IDEA statute does not prohibit the participation of counsel at IEP meetings, the IDEA statute makes clear that such involvement is *discouraged*. Human nature being what it is, there is a feeling that some attorneys (other than the attorneys in my office, of course!) will feel compelled to "posture" and advocate rather than assist the process of developing consensus and closure.

When parents (or school districts for that matter) bring attorneys to the IEP table, the presence of counsel often serves to "chill" the discussion. With an attorney present, school district personnel (unless also represented by counsel at the IEP meeting) become very quiet, and say only what they need to say. This is not the quality of open dialogue that is necessary to develop an appropriate IEP.

When parents bring attorneys to the IEP table, even if counsel is attending only as an observer, some school district may attempt to blame the parents' counsel at any future due process proceeding for any procedural safeguard defect that was not specifically targeted for remediation by the child's counsel at the IEP meeting. While we do not consider it the obligation of the child's counsel to help the school district remediate its procedural errors, it still may put the child's counsel in a most uncomfortable position to the extent that they are asked to explain why he or she did not previously raise procedural violations that were not raised at the IEP.

In view of the IDEA statute, which discourages the attendance of counsel at IEP meetings, it is our recommendation that parents be <u>prepared</u> by counsel to attend the IEP meeting, but that counsel *not* attend. There is no duty on the part of parents to disclose to the school district that counsel has been retained. If any surprises or unanticipated logjams should come up at the IEP meeting, parents can always request a five minute break and then call counsel privately on a cell phone for advice and feedback.

Parents have the fear that if counsel is not present, they will be made to sign things that they do not wish to sign. The simple answer is that except for an "attendance form," or perhaps consent for an evaluation, parents should never sign *anything* at the IEP meeting itself.

Even if the IEP document being presented to parents is thought to represent the perfect educational placement and program, parents should ask for a copy of the proposed IEP or other document, and offer to get back to the IEP team within 24, 48 or 72 hours (after having a reasonable opportunity to consult with counsel). There is no downside to being cautious and prudent, and a more careful review often reveals mistakes and flaws that even the school district did not intend.

<u>When the Child Has To Raise the "Village"</u>: In her book, "It Takes A Village," Senator Hillary Rodham Clinton popularized an African proverb to acknowledge the "full court press" that is necessary to educate ***typically*** developed children. It is axiomatic that more extensive and comprehensive support systems are required to properly raise and educate children with disabilities.

We have represented families in more than two-dozen states, as far away as Alaska. From time to time, even in high-density urban areas, the school district will acknowledge that it does not have personnel with the special expertise needed to address certain needs. Sometimes, the issue is finding an experienced oral-motor specialist for a child with motor planning problems. Sometimes, a school district has never dealt with a genuine behavior analyst (board certified or otherwise), and has relied exclusively on the expertise of a school psychologist to develop functional behavioral assessments/analyses and behavior intervention plans.

Sometimes, it takes the needs of a single child to get the school district to seek out and engage the special resources that are necessary to support the child. Those resources are then established not only for the benefit of the individual child, but also for the benefit of children to follow. Parents often are the sleuths who do the required due diligence to come up with the names of these professionals. This brings up another point.

At the IEP level, particularly if the school district is agreeing to hire them, parents should never make a point of complaining to the school district that they (the child's parents) were the ones who found the necessary providers. What good can possibly come from embarrassing the school district's administrator in this manner? In fact, what difference is it if the school district administrator takes all the credit for finding the providers? After all, you *want* the school district to be genuinely invested in your child's program.

"Chains, chains, shackles and chains
No matter what it takes, some day I'm gonna break these
Chains, chains, shackles and chains...."

Patty Loveless

Chapter 9

The Thorny Issue of "Least Restrictive Environment"

One of the greatest challenges facing most children and adolescents with disabilities is being meaningfully successful in the context of less restrictive educational settings. These settings can run the spectrum from integrated, collaborative models to full-blown mainstreaming i.e. a class where the rest of the class consists of typically developed children.

The challenge, when executed correctly, typically involves a relentless "full court press" by parents, educators and administrators. There are legal, as well as practical, considerations, that parents and school district personnel alike should be aware of.

The Salient Legal Considerations: Congress has adopted a clear preference for educating children with disabilities in their least restrictive environment. There is no wooden test to be applied and what is the least restrictive environment for one child may not be the least restrictive environment for another child. The statutory mandate is that school districts are required to ensure "that to *the maximum extent appropriate,* children with disabilities, including children in public or private institutions or other care facilities, are educated with children who are non-disabled." (20 U.S.C. Sec. 1412(a)(5). There is a similar mandate to provide the child with access to the general curriculum (to the "maximum extent appropriate").

There is no requirement that children with disabilities have to "earn" the right to a less restrictive setting. Congress has placed the onus on school districts to ensure that children with disabilities are given the supports that they may need to be successful in their least restrictive environment.

Congress also has *presupposed* that children with disabilities may need a one-to-one support aide as well as other supports and accommodations to be successful in an inclusion or mainstream environment. In this regard, school districts are unconditionally required to ensure "that special classes, separate schooling or other removal of children with disabilities from the regular educational environment occurs *only* if the nature or severity of the disability is such that education in regular classes <u>with the use of supplementary aids and services</u> cannot be achieved satisfactorily."

The foregoing mandate thus serves as a stop sign for school districts that are proposing to move children into more restrictive settings unless they have done what can be done to keep the child in the less restrictive setting. The practical problem is that school districts that want to move a child into a more restrictive setting will attempt to rely on a few isolated incidents of inappropriate behavior and then claim that the child simply cannot be maintained and educated in the less restrictive setting. How can parents hope to offer evidence to the contrary and persuade the school district to "try harder?"

To prevent this kind of situation from becoming an overwhelming force, the first thing that parents need is an early warning system. In this regard, a daily "Communication Book" that goes back and forth from school to home can be critical. Even without the collection of data on target behaviors (for those children who do not start the school year with a behavior plan in place), informal monthly meetings with the classroom teacher can be helpful. To check the "pulse" of the educational setting from time to time, parents may also want to speak informally with some of the other parents.

At the first hint of any significant behavioral difficulty, parents should write a letter to the school district and insist on getting a behavior analyst and/or educational consultant into the classroom to observe and assess the child's behaviors. Once again, the issue of who would be paying for this observation/assessment is secondary.

With the benefit of a classroom observation, behavior analysts and educational consultants often will come up with additional and/or different strategies and recommendations that the school district has not yet tried. Ferreting out these additional and different strategies and recommendations can be critical because, as noted above, the statutory language says that the school district may not recommend a more restrictive setting unless the school district first exercises the due diligence to show that even with supports, aides and accommodations, the child cannot be maintained in the less restrictive setting. In essence, the behavior analyst or educational consultant can help a parent create the road map that the district has not yet tried.

The same statutory language also means that school districts <u>cannot</u> arbitrarily bar access to inclusion or mainstream settings on the basis that "the child would need a one-to one aide." Indeed, before the school district may even consider a more restrictive setting, the school district must demonstrably exercise due diligence to show that even with supplementary aids and services, the child *cannot* be successful in the less restrictive setting.[29]

The concept of "least restrictive environment" means just that. For this reason, some federal courts have recognized and held that, for example, an "integrated" preschool setting is more restrictive than a full-blown "mainstream" preschool setting. Both settings *include* non-disabled peers, but it is the mainstream setting that is considered "least" restrictive because the class (except, of course, for the one child with the eligible disability), consists entirely of non-disabled peers.

An Important Caveat: *The Comment following 34 Code of Federal Regulations, Section 300.550-556, states, however, that the presumption in favor of mainstreaming may be overcome upon a showing that "a handicapped child is so disruptive in a regular classroom that the education of other students is significantly impaired [because] the needs of the handicapped child cannot be met in that environment."*

The least restrictive environment mandate is <u>not</u> an absolute. The other children in the class have educational rights that must be taken into account.

---

[29] Even today, many school districts are still confused about the concept of "least restrictive environment," and what that means for the school district. Too many school districts will erroneously advise parents at the IEP meeting, "Well, if Jennifer needs a one-to-one support aide to be successful in a mainstream setting, she is not *ready* for that kind of setting and should remain in a self-contained setting." The express language set forth in the IDEA statute shows that Congress wisely understood that it is too much to expect 100% readiness, and that school districts must be prepared to supply appropriate supports, aides and accommodations to help the child succeed in the less restrictive setting. This can include not only supports and accommodations in the classroom itself, but extended day (after school) programming.

Of course, even in a situation where a child with a disability is wreaking havoc in the classroom, it might be incumbent upon the school district to show that it had exercised due diligence to try to maintain the child in the mainstream setting (e.g. the school district had tried the support of a behavioral consultant, functional behavioral analysis, behavior intervention plan, behaviorally trained 1:1 support aide, and had even approved extended day interventions at home).

Example: All too often, the parent of a child with behavioral issues will be called by the school to "come and pick up" their child. Where the function of the child's behavior is task avoidance, this kind of situation, particularly if repeated, creates a scenario where the child is actually getting rewarded and reinforced for inappropriate behavior. Where Johnny's objective is to avoid work and go home, Johnny quickly learns that if he kicks or bites another student, he will soon get his wish! The very first of such telephone calls is a "red flag" to a parent that it is time to bring in a qualified and experienced behavioral consultant.

Today, while not absolutely essential in most states, a fairly good indicator of special behavioral expertise is a professional who has successfully gone through the regimen of becoming a "Board Certified Behavior Analyst."

In recent years, some school districts have seized upon "least restrictive environment" in an effort to justify placing children with severe disabilities in mainstream settings with the least amount of support (and cost). At the very least, this kind of situation represents educational neglect and a deprivation of the right to an appropriate education. At its worst, it can represent a form of child abuse.

Some school districts cling to the view that so long as the child is not hurting anyone, the child should be in a mainstream setting. While it is seductive for parents of children with disabilities to hear that the school district is recommending a mainstream setting, parents must ask themselves the hard question of whether their child is arguably appropriate for such a setting. That is precisely why Congress used the phrase "maximum extent *appropriate*."

If a child is merely sharing the same oxygen as the other children, and is not able to make good and meaningful progress in the mainstream setting, even with the benefit of supports, aides and accommodations, parents should be pressing the school district to explore other settings and options that will promote meaningful educational progress.

Parents and school districts alike need to keep in mind that Congress enacted the mandate of "least restrictive environment" to *protect* children with disabilities, not to throw them into the deep end of the swimming pool before they have developed any of the requisite swimming skill sets.

Functional Behavioral Assessments and Behavior Plans: Many school psychologists apparently have their school districts convinced that they know how to do a functional behavioral assessment ("FBA") and how to develop a Behavioral Intervention Plan ("BIP") based on the results of the FBA.

In actuality, very few school psychologists have the training or experience to develop appropriate FBA's or effective BIP's. It is embarrassing for the school district when these same school psychologists appear at due process hearings and are not even able to define basic behavior terms. Except in the unusual case where the school district's psychologist has had the training and experience of a behavior analyst, this is one area where school districts are best served bringing in an outside consultant.

Many school districts will make the mistake of developing a BIP, and then treating the BIP as if it were written in stone, never to be changed again. Experienced behavior analysts know that children's behaviors often *change* quickly over time, and for this reason, the BIP needs to be revisited and revised frequently. Unfortunately, we have litigated many due process cases where the evidence showed that a BIP developed by the school district promptly developed *rigor mortis*, never to be changed again.

Even where everything goes *right*, and an appropriate BIP has been developed, it is essential that all school district staff and the child's parents receive adequate instruction and training in its appropriate *implementation*.

Many times, it turns out that the BIP has been shown only to the classroom teacher, and <u>not</u> the child's classroom support aide or the child's parents. This kind of situation injects unhelpful uncertainty, inconsistency and unpredictability into the behavioral dynamic, and virtually guarantees that there will be no meaningful remediation of the target behaviors. When an appropriate BIP has been developed, it is essential to get everyone involved with the child on the same page. Consistency is absolutely critical.

Selecting and Caring For the One-To-One Support Aide: It is comforting for many parents that a 1:1 support aide has been written into their child's IEP but at best, that is only a first step.   There is something bizarre and ironic about the fact that what often is the most important teaching instrument in the classroom usually is the worst paid and also usually has been given the least amount of training.

Freshly minted soldiers can expect to have received at least five or six weeks of "basic training." For some reason, however, most of the nation's school districts have the idea that one or two days of an "in-service training" will be sufficient training for support aides who may well be encountering highly challenging—and sometimes dangerous—situations and behaviors.

In the absence of an interfering collective bargaining agreement, it often is possible to finesse the situation where the school district hires someone from the child's "home program" to serve as the child's classroom aide. Absent an agreement, however, it is difficult, if next to impossible, to *compel* the school district to do so. Hearing officers do not assume the authority to hire or fire personnel. They do have the power, however, to declare that school district personnel are lacking in the experience or training needed to appropriately support the child at issue.

Preserving The LRE Setting In the Event of A Dispute: Assume that your child is attending a mainstream kindergarten setting without an aide, BIP or other supports and at your child's annual review, the school district announces that the year has not gone well, and that because of your child's disruptive behaviors, they are going to be recommending a more restrictive, self-contained class. Further assume that the school district says that it does not intend to try a one-to-one aide or any other supports, and that if your child needs these additional supports, he or she needs to be in a more "structured" (translation: more restrictive) setting.

At the IEP meeting, you might be able to induce a change of heart by advising the school district that the recommended change is not acceptable, and that if you receive an IEP recommending a more restrictive setting, you probably will retain counsel to file for due process and invoke "pendency." Pendency (sometimes also known as "stay put") is a powerful tool than is invoked by filing for due process. In essence, invoking statutory pendency will serve to preserve the existing *status quo* at least until the due process case can be adjudicated.

If the school district persists with an unduly restrictive recommendation, it is important to understand that the statutory right of pendency is not automatic and that it is not actually invoked until such time as there has been a *filing* for due process.

All the links in the chain pulled together,
and the chain became unbreakable.

George S. Patton

Chapter 10

Making the Case for "Extended School Year" and "Extended Day" Services

The IDEA statute and its implementing regulations expressly make provision for extended school year ("ESY") services; that is, services that are delivered beyond the confines of the regular school year. The IDEA statute also makes provision for "extended day" services; that is, services that are delivered outside of the time frame of the regular school day.

Parents often are surprised to find out that they are "allowed" to ask for extended school year and extended day services. These same parents are even more surprised when they find out about other, similarly situated children who already are receiving these kinds of supplemental supports and services.

The fact that this supplemental educational programming is written right into the IDEA statute makes it clear enough that Congress fully intended such programming to be *considered* as part of the "full continuum." However, the fact that these additional supports are available for consideration does not necessarily mean automatic entitlement. As one might anticipate, just as is the case with other programming decisions, the recognized litmus test is needs-driven.

Extended School Year Services: In the case of ESY services, a case for entitlement is made out where it is reasonably anticipated that going without ESY services would translate to *significant* regression that would not be easily recouped. Essentially, there would be a functional loss of skills acquired during the regular school year.

While evidence of actual regression certainly will help make out the case for ESY services, the mere *anticipation* of significant regression can suffice. Thus, there is no requirement that your child actually fail in a full-blown regression before being approved for ESY services. Once your child drowns, it is a little late for life preservers.

How then, can parents demonstrate that going without ESY services would likely result in a significant regression for their child that would not be easily recouped?

Typically, ESY decisions are made during the annual review IEP meeting that normally takes place near the end of the school year. To the extent not already provided to the school district, this is the time for parents to come forward with whatever evidence they may have to demonstrate that ESY programming is both necessary and appropriate i.e. that the failure to provide ESY programming would likely result in a significant regression that would not be easily recouped.

Since most states do not require school districts to provide more than a "free and appropriate public education"(FAPE), it is important for parents to keep in mind that the case for ESY services will not be made out where providing the ESY program would simply be "better" or "more appropriate." To put it another way, where the provision of services during the regular school year would itself be sufficient to provide the student with a FAPE, there really is no entitlement to ESY services.

Just as is the case with securing services during the regular school year, it is important for parents pressing for ESY services to depersonalize the request. Requests for ESY services are likely to be better received if supported by meaningful "regression statements;" that is, the written opinions of professionals having some meaningful personal experience with the child attesting to the anticipated threat of significant regression that would not be easily recouped.

In addition to securing regression statements secured from knowledgeable professionals who are familiar with the child, parents can further support the need for ESY programming by collecting and presenting data reflecting incidents of actual regression where significant "recoup" time was required. It can provide a compelling window of insight to show what happened to a child's academic programming or behavioral data following an extended school vacation, staff departures or other hiatus periods.

Even after the school district agrees that ESY services are warranted, parents need to continue to be vigilant to ensure that their child receives a sufficient *level* of ESY programming.

Generally, the pertinent inquiry is what it will take for the child to *maintain* and not lose the skills that were learned during the school year. Some children, however, particularly children diagnosed with autism who may require fast-paced and flexible programming, may stagnate and then quickly lose skills and acquire (or reacquire) behaviors with an approach that does not allow for regular modifications to programming. Another possible exception to the general rule is the child who happens to end the school year at a "critical juncture" in his or her program.

Parents should ask the school district to delineate precisely what kind of services will be provided, and when such services will be provided. When children are approved for a "twelve month" program of ESY services, it is important to find out the extent of any "breaks" in the programming. Many school districts, for example, will offer ESY services for only six weeks during the summer. While these school districts will defend such programs by using terms such as "state mandated," what this really means is that the school district would be in violation of state law if it offered even a minute less than the six week program. If your child truly needs the extra time, it is not unheard of for students to receive seven or eight weeks of ESY programming during the summer. Depending on need, some students will qualify for a full summer of programming.

Extended Day Services: Many school districts will take the position that they have a practice or policy that all teaching and programming must be delivered in school during the regular school day, between Monday and Friday. This is a perfectly fine practice, unless your child happens to be a child whose individual needs go beyond the regular school day. If additional services over and above those provided during the regular school day are required to provide your child with a FAPE, your child is a good candidate for extended day services.

Extended day services may be delivered in a variety of venues, including home, school, and office locations. There is nothing in the IDEA statute that precludes extended day services from being delivered on the weekends, or even on holidays.

The following factors are among those that would militate in favor of qualifying a student for extended day programming:

✔ The student who requires a great deal of pre-teaching and/or re-teaching

✔ The student who exhibits significant "interfering behaviors" in class

✔ The student who has significant difficulty generalizing skills

✔ The student who would be practicing and rehearsing stereotypical or other inappropriate behaviors within a non-structured environment

✔ The student who demonstrably regresses and requires "recoup" time even after an intervening weekend

✔ The student who needs the support of extended day programming to help support their continued success in a least restrictive environment setting (i.e. a mainstream or inclusion setting)

✔ The student who needs the support of extended day programming to promote the child's education with non-disabled peers, to the "maximum extent appropriate" (i.e. the applicable standard under the IDEA statute)

Just as with other services and supports, it is essential that parents present the request for ESY and/or extended day programming at the IEP meeting. Once such a request is made, it is then incumbent upon the school district to act upon it and, if the request is rejected, such rejection must be coupled with a rationale and justification. Parents faced with a rejection of a request for ESY or extended day programming should preserve their right to seek reimbursement and other relief with appropriate notice to the school district. Here is an example of a letter parents can adapt where the school district has rejected a request for *ESY* programming:

Dear [IEP Chairperson, with copy to case manager]:

In view of the regression statements provided to the district by our son's speech, ABA and OT providers at the annual review IEP meeting, we are most disappointed that the district has refused to offer our son any

ESY programming. Our son clearly needs significant ESY programming to prevent a material regression that would not be easily recouped.

In light of our son's documented needs, we must respectfully put the district on notice that we intend to provide our son with appropriate ESY programming as recommended in the regression statements, and that we intend to look to the district to reimburse us to the extent of our costs and expenses in this regard.

As we indicated at the IEP meeting, we would have accepted a seven week ESY program to reach an amicable resolution of this issue. However, since we were not able to come to amicable compromise on ESY issues, we intend to provide ESY programming for the full ten week time frame that is being recommended by our son's professionals.

Sincerely,

Here is an example of a "ten day notice" where the school district has rejected a request for any *extended day* programming:

Dear [IEP Chairperson, with copy to case manager]

We are disappointed that the district rejected our request for any extended day programming for our son Alex. Our son needs this additional programming to support his meaningful success and progress in his mainstream educational placement, and to promote generalization of learned skills. The provision of extended day programming for Alex's [e.g. 1:1 ABA, speech and language services, occupational therapy, etc.] helps to ensure that Alex will maximize his educational experience with non-disabled peers. The district's proposal to continuously pull Alex out of his classroom for 1:1 instruction time ensures just the opposite.

In light of the above, we must put the district on notice that we intend to proceed to secure appropriate extended day services for Alex, including consultation and team meeting time, and that we intend to look to the district to reimburse us for our costs.

Sincerely,

Finally, set forth below is a further variation on the same theme, where the school district has agreed to provide *some* ESY services, but where the school district's offer is inadequate and inappropriate:

Dear [Chairperson]:

We are in receipt of the district's proposed IEP for our son Alex for the upcoming summer time frame.

Given our son's unique needs, we do not consider the district's offer of three hours per week of ESY programming to be adequate or appropriate. Please be advised that we intend to accept the three hours on a "without prejudice" basis and that we intend to supplement these hours with additional service hours, along the lines recommended in the regression statements submitted by Alex's existing service providers.

To the extent that we incur costs to fulfill these additional service hours, we intend to look to the district for reimbursement.

Sincerely,

I am not a teacher but an awakener.

Robert Frost

Chapter 11

Psychopharmacology 101

Pharmacological intervention is a delicate subject. So many different factors are at play.

In the first instance, parents will hear and read about lots of other children who are taking "meds" and will wonder if they are making a huge mistake if their child is not among them. When parents hear anecdotal reports of success stories involving meds, inquiry should be made by these same parents to find out what *other* interventions the child in question has been receiving. Invariably, there will be quite a few other interventions going on.

Some school districts looking for a quick fix in the name of behavior management will waste no time suggesting to parents that their child needs the support of pharmacological interventions. Typically, the child's teacher may say something like "Joshua has had a really rough couple of weeks. Is he taking any kind of meds? No? Have you considered any?"

Parents should understand that there is a world of difference between behavior *management* and behavior *modification*. Before rushing headlong into pharmacology (because of pressure from the school district or other sources), parents should make sure that at the very least, they have given serious consideration to other measures (e.g. the support of a behavior consultant, a functional behavioral assessment, a behavior intervention plan, etc.)

The issue is not about being in favor or against pharmacological intervention. Pharmacology should be viewed as a needs-based intervention. If after genuinely trying other available methods, pharmacological intervention is pretty much the only thing that will help your child maintain the attention and focus that your child needs to be meaningfully and qualitatively "available" for learning, parents should by all means give consideration to this avenue.

While one or more pharmacological interventions may enhance your child's focus and attentiveness and general availability for learning, it is important to keep in mind that there are no "magic silver bullets." Accordingly, when implementing a pharmacological intervention, it is essential to maintain all of the other educational supports and interventions, at least those that are demonstrably effective.

Parents need to know that the impact of pharmacological intervention often will *vary* from child to child. The same is true with respect to possible "side effects." As with everything else, an individualized approach is absolutely essential. It is therefore an "absolute" that parents should not dream of pursuing a pharmacological intervention without the support, supervision and care of a medical doctor with significant prior experience and training in this area.

The fact that a doctor has a *license* to prescribe meds, however, does not necessarily mean that the doctor has the requisite experience to dispense or monitor them. Accordingly, if you are considering meds for your child, ask your child's pediatric developmental specialist what, if any experience he or she has had in the area, and specifically, what "track record" he or she has seen with the particular pharmacological approach that is being recommended for your child.

Parents also should ask what plans the pediatric developmental specialist has for monitoring and, if necessary, modifying the use of meds. A *systematic* monitoring approach is considered essential. Parents should be wary of cavalier recommendations that sound like "Let's try this and see how it goes."

When meds are being implemented in a school setting, it is important to enlist the support of school personnel in the monitoring process. Just as it is important for the school district to take data on your child's behaviors, it is important for the school district to take monitoring data when implementing a pharmacological regimen. Ask your prescribing physician for a monitoring form that you can ask the school district to fill out and return on a regular basis.

The time to repair the roof is when the sun is shining.

John F. Kennedy

Chapter 12

School Discipline

An entire book could be devoted to the evolving world of school discipline, and the laws, statutes, regulations and principles that will be applicable when, as is all too often the case, a child with a disability is charged as the offending party.

Parents can and normally should go to most IEP meetings without counsel. Parents typically can even go to mediation without counsel. The prospect of significant school discipline, on the other hand, is an entirely different and far more serious matter because of the potential for immediate and extreme consequences. In an abundance of caution, when a school district imposes or threatens to impose a significant disciplinary sanction, it is time to consult with counsel

In the wake of the shootings in Columbine, the Mepham High School football scandal, and other chilling incidents, the theme these days clearly is one of "zero tolerance." These days, a one-day suspension from school can easily mushroom into a much longer suspension, or even into an expulsion. Inertia and momentum are powerful physical forces. Where the circumstances surrounding and precipitating the behaviors at issue are allowed to continue, it is just a matter of time before the behavior will resurface.[30]

---

[30] By way of example, we have seen time and again the unfortunate situation of a children being routinely placed in "time out" for inappropriate behavior. For those children who are engaged in "task avoidance," the time out imposed by the school district inadvertently serves as a potent reward and "reinforcer." We have often seen the behaviors of these children *worsen* the more time outs they receive. Another variation on this theme is the problem of school districts that rush to call parents to "pick up your child from school" the moment that the child engages in an inappropriate behavior. Unfortunately, school districts that take the easy way out pave the way for these children to quickly learn that the faster they kick or bite a classmate, the faster mommy will arrive to take them home.

Ideally, school discipline is something that can be anticipated and *prevented* by employment of prophylactic measures. At the very least, when school discipline is imposed, it is something that must be dealt with (and remedied) by parents on an "early intervention" basis.

In general, special needs children who engage in inappropriate behavior will be entitled to special treatment if the alleged misconduct is found to be *related* to his or her disability. Generally, this is a determination that the school district will make at a "manifestation hearing." Under the current IDEA statute,[31] a student's behavior will <u>not</u> be considered related to the disability provided that the school district establishes <u>each</u> of the following:

✔ The student's IEP and placement were appropriate (in relation to the behavior subject to sanction);

✔ The special education services, supplementary aids and services, and intervention strategies were provided consistent with the IEP and placement (i.e. there were no material IEP fulfillment issues);

✔ The student's disability did not impair the ability of the student to *understand* the impact and consequences of the behavior subject to disciplinary action;

✔ The child's disability did not impair the ability of the child to *control* the behavior that is the subject of disciplinary action.

Accordingly, when problematic behaviors surface, it is essential that these behaviors be identified as being a manifestation of (i.e. related to) your child's disability and/or a faulty IEP. Drawing that kind of connection is necessary to ensure that your child is given special treatment and consideration. For example, as a general matter, a student with a disability cannot be suspended for more than 10 (school) days if the offending conduct and behavior was caused by or was related to his or her disability.

Prophylactic Measures: In preceding chapters, we have noted the importance of targeting and conducting a functional behavioral assessment of behaviors that would be anticipated to interfere with the child's learning, or the learning of others. Read as a

---

[31] 34 C.F.R. Sec. 300.523.

whole, the federal IDEA statute communicates that school districts should be considering and implementing behavior intervention plans for students with disabilities long *before* the situation escalates into a suspension or longer term removal. Clearly, prophylactic measures are called for.

If your child presents with problematic behaviors, how, if at all, are those behaviors identified in your child's IEP? To the extent that your child presents with potentially problematic behaviors, does your child need the support of a behaviorally trained one-to-one aide? If so, has your school district secured appropriate and regularly scheduled supervision and consultation services from an experienced behavior analyst? Similarly, does your child need social skills training delivered at school and/or on an extended day (after school) basis? Does your child have appropriate social, communication and behavior goals and objectives written into his or her IEP? Do you maintain regular communication with your child's teacher through meetings and/or through the use of a daily "communication book?"

Make sure to ask for these supports if there is any evidence that they are warranted in your child's case. If the school district refuses to implement the very supports, aides and accommodations that your child needs, and you make an appropriate record, that same record will help you later in the event that the school district seeks to impose school discipline.

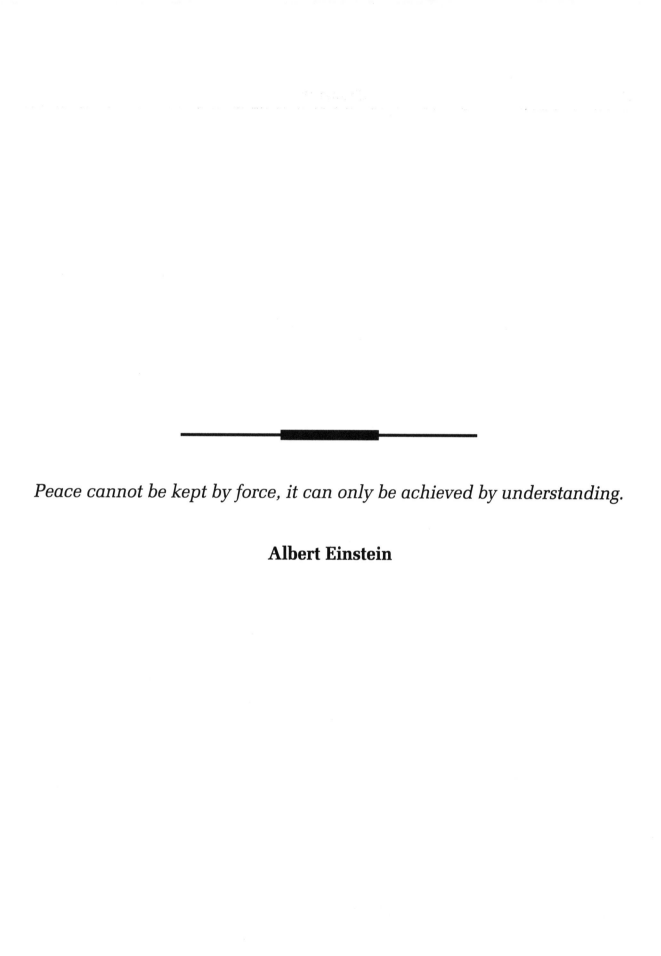

Peace cannot be kept by force, it can only be achieved by understanding.

Albert Einstein

Chapter 13

The Mediation Process

If, after all your efforts, you are locked in a dispute with your local school district that must be resolved, you may want to consider non-binding mediation before you proceed to a due process hearing, where there would be an actual adjudication after the administrative equivalent of a trial. Typically, mediation is an informal and relatively brief process that does not necessarily have to involve the engagement of legal counsel.

The benefit of mediation is that if it is successful, you will avoid the expense and burden of going to an impartial hearing ("due process"). In some states, such as New York, going to mediation in the context of services being provided by "early intervention" is a near-absolute prerequisite and condition to having "standing" to collect attorneys' fees later, if you ultimately do decide to go to due process.

There are, however, at least two potential "downsides" of going to mediation. First, there is the obvious issue of delay. If you have a time-sensitive issue, you probably cannot afford the risk that the mediation will be unsuccessful. That is precisely why the IDEA statute promotes the concept of mediation, but also provides that the option of mediation cannot be used to delay parents who wish to go to an impartial hearing.

The other risk of going to mediation is that the school district may have no genuine interest in proceeding to mediation except to conduct informal "discovery" for purposes of the main event i.e. the impartial hearing.

If you decide to proceed to mediation, the first thing you should do is make sure that everyone has signed a standard form that provides that nothing said at the mediation may be referred to or used by the parties in the event that the mediation is unsuccessful, and the matter proceeds to an impartial hearing.

If you proceed to mediation without the benefit of counsel, and you are able to reach seeming agreement with the school district, it normally is a good idea to have the mediation agreement reviewed by counsel before you sign it. Often, an attorney will be able to objectively focus on provisions, terminology or omissions that can cause problems later on. Once you sign a mediation agreement, it is very difficult to be relieved of its consequences, even if your child's needs change during the time frame of the agreement.

Resources

Department of Education

Alabama
http://www.alsde.edu/html/home.asp

Alaska
http://www.eed.state.ak.us/

Arizona
http://www.ade.state.az.us/

Arkansas
http://arkedu.state.ar.us/

California
http://www.cde.ca.gov/

Colorado
http://www.cde.state.co.us/

Connecticut
http://www.state.ct.us/sde/

Delaware
http://www.doe.state.de.us/

District of Columbia
http://www.k12.dc.us/dcps/home.html

Florida
http://www.fldoe.org/Default.asp?bhcp=1

Georgia
http://www.doe.k12.ga.us/index.asp

Hawaii
http://www.k12.hi.us/

Idaho
http://www.sde.state.id.us/Dept/

Indiana
http://www.doe.state.in.us/

Iowa
http://www.state.ia.us/educate/

Kansas
http://www.ksde.org/

Kentucky
http://www.kentuckyschools.org/

Louisiana
http://www.louisianaschools.net/lde/index.html

Maine
http://www.state.me.us/education/homepage.htm

Maryland
http://www.marylandpublicschools.org/MSDE

Massachusetts
http://www.doe.mass.edu/

Michigan
http://www.michigan.gov/mde/

Minnesota
http://education.state.mn.us/html/mde_home.htm

Mississippi
http://www.mde.k12.ms.us/

Missouri
http://dese.mo.gov/

Montana
http://www.opi.state.mt.us/

Nebraska
http://www.nde.state.ne.us/

Nevada
http://www.doe.nv.gov/

New Hampshire
http://www.ed.state.nh.us/

New Jersey
http://www.state.nj.us/education/

New Mexico
http://www.sde.state.nm.us/

New York
http://www.nysed.gov/

North Carolina
http://www.ncpublicschools.org/

North Dakota
http://www.dpi.state.nd.us/

Ohio
http://www.ode.state.oh.us/

Oklahoma
http://sde.state.ok.us/home/defaultie.html

Oregon
http://www.ode.state.or.us/

Pennsylvania
http://www.pde.state.pa.us/pde_internet/site/default.asp

Rhode Island
http://www.ridoe.net/

South Carolina
http://www.myscschools.com/

South Dakota
http://www.state.sd.us/deca/

Tennessee
http://www.state.tn.us/education/

Texas
http://www.tea.state.tx.us/

Utah
http://www.usoe.k12.ut.us/

Vermont
http://www.state.vt.us/educ/

Virginia
http://www.pen.k12.va.us/go/VDOE/

Washington
http://www.k12.wa.us/

West Virginia
http://wvde.state.wv.us/

Wisconsin
http://www.dpi.state.wi.us/

Wyoming
http://www.k12.wy.us/index.asp

TERRITORIES

Puerto Rico
http://www.gobierno.pr/GPRPortal/Inicio/EducacionEInvestigacion/DE.htm

Virgin Islands
http://www.usvi.org/education/

Guam
http://www.doe.edu.gu/

Northern Mariana Is.
http://www.pss.cnmi.mp/PSSCentralOffice/index.cfm?pageID=1

ADDITIONAL RESOURCES – NATIONAL

US Department of Education
http://www.ed.gov/index.jhtml

Early Intervention

STATE/
WEBSITE ADDRESS

Alabama
http://www.rehab.state.al.us/Home/default.aspx?url=/Home/Services/AEIS/Main&flash=yes

Alaska
http://health.hss.state.ak.us/ocs/InfantLearning/default.htm

Arizona
http://www.de.state.az.us/azeip/default.asp

Arkansas
http://www.state.ar.us/dhs/ddds/FirstConn/index.html

California
http://www.dds.ca.gov/EarlyStart/ESHome.cfm

Colorado
http://www.cde.state.co.us/earlychildhoodconnections/

Connecticut
http://www.birth23.org/

Delaware
http://www.state.de.us/dhss/dms/epqc/birth3/directry.html

District of Columbia
http://dhs.dc.gov/dhs/cwp/view.asp?a=3&Q=492390&dhsNAV=%7C30989%7C

Florida
http://www.cms-kids.com/InfantHome.htm

Georgia
http://www.ph.dhr.state.ga.us/programs/bcw/index.shtml

Hawaii
http://www.nal.usda.gov/pavnet/fp/fphawaii.htm

Idaho
http://www2.state.id.us/dhw/InfToddler/index.htm

Indiana
http://www.eikids.com/matrix/default.asp

Iowa
http://www.state.ia.us/educate/ecese/cfcs/ea/index.html

Kansas
http://www.kdhe.state.ks.us/its/

Kentucky
http://www.education.ky.gov/KDE/Instructional+Resources/Early+Childhood+Development/
default.htm

Louisiana
http://www.oph.dhh.state.la.us/childrensspecial/earlyinterventionservices/index.html

Maine
http://www.maine.gov/education/speced/cdsstaff.htm

Maryland
http://cte.jhu.edu/dse_eis/eis.cfm

Massachusetts
http://www.mass.gov/dph/fch/ei.htm

Michigan
http://www.earlyonmichigan.org/

Minnesota
http://education.state.mn.us/html/intro_speced_eci.htm

Mississippi
http://www.msdh.state.ms.us/msdhsite/index.cfm/32,0,74,html

Missouri
http://dese.mo.gov/divspeced/FirstSteps/

Montana
http://www.dphhs.state.mt.us/dsd/

Nebraska
http://www.nde.state.ne.us/ECH/ECH.html

Nevada
http://health2k.state.nv.us/BEIS/

New Hampshire
http://nhdds.org/programs/famchild/earlysupports/

New Jersey
http://www.njeis.org/

New Mexico
http://164.64.166.11/cilt/programs/ece/

New York
http://www.health.state.ny.us/nysdoh/eip/index.htm

North Carolina
http://www.ncei.org/ei/itp.html

North Dakota
http://ndearlyintervention.com/dhs/eip.nsf/ParentInfo?OpenView

Ohio
http://www.odh.state.oh.us/ODHPrograms/EI/earlyint1.htm

Oklahoma
http://sde.state.ok.us/home/defaultie.html

Oregon
http://www.ode.state.or.us/sped/spedareas/eiesce/index.htm

Pennsylvania
http://www.pde.state.pa.us/special_edu/cwp/
view.asp?a=177&Q=61687&g=214&special_eduNav=|3902|3914|&special_eduNav=|2199|&specialeduNav=|3899|2199|

Rhode Island
http://www.healthri.org/family/ei/Home.htm

South Carolina
http://www.scdhec.net/babynet/

South Dakota
http://www.state.sd.us/deca/Special/Birthto3/index.htm

Tennessee
http://www.state.tn.us/education/teishome.htm

Texas
http://www.eci.state.tx.us/

Utah
http://www.utahbabywatch.org/

Vermont
http://www.healthyvermonters.info/hi/cshn/fitp/fitp.shtml

Virginia
http://www.infantva.org/

Washington
http://www1.dshs.wa.gov/iteip/index.html

West Virginia
http://www.wvdhhr.org/birth23/

Wisconsin
http://dhfs.wisconsin.gov/bdds/birthto3/

Wyoming
http://ddd.state.wy.us/Documents/mitch1.htm

TERRITORIES

Puerto Rico
http://www.salud.gov.pr/Divisiones/Servicios%20Habilitacion.htm

Virgin Islands
http://www.uconnced.org/map/virginislands.htm

Guam
http://www.doe.edu.gu/sped/GEIS%20Index.htm

Northern Mariana Is.
http://www.pss.cnmi.mp/PSSCentralOffice/index.cfm?pageID=55

ADDITIONAL RESOURCES – NATIONAL

National Early Childhood Technical Assistance Center
http://www.nectac.org/search/confinder.asp

Special Education Services

STATE/
WEBSITE ADDRESS

Alabama
http://www.alsde.edu/html/sections/section_detail.asp?section=65&footer=sections

Alaska
http://www.eed.state.ak.us/tls/sped/

Arizona
http://www.ade.state.az.us/ess/ESSHome.asp

Arkansas
http://arkedu.state.ar.us/directory/accountability_p2.html

California
http://www.cde.ca.gov/sp/se/

Colorado
http://www.cde.state.co.us/index_special.htm

Connecticut
http://www.state.ct.us/sde/deps/special/index.htm

Delaware
http://www.doe.state.de.us/programs/specialed/

District of Columbia
http://www.k12.dc.us/dcps/specialed/dcpsspecedhome.html

Florida
http://www.firn.edu/doe/commhome/

Georgia
http://www.doe.k12.ga.us/curriculum/exceptional/index.asp

Hawaii
http://doe.k12.hi.us/specialeducation/

Idaho
http://www.sde.state.id.us/SpecialEd/

Indiana
http://ideanet.doe.state.in.us/exceptional/speced/welcome.html

Iowa
http://www.state.ia.us/educate/ecese/cfcs/speced/index.html

Kansas
http://sssweb.ksde.org/kansped/

Kentucky
http://www.kentuckyschools.org/KDE/Instructional+Resources/Student+and+Family+Support/
Exceptional+Children/default.htm

Louisiana
http://www.louisianaschools.net/lde/specialp/home.html

Maine
http://www.maine.gov/education/speced/specserv.htm

Maryland
http://www.marylandpublicschools.org/MSDE/divisions/earlyinterv/

Massachusetts
http://www.doe.mass.edu/sped/

Michigan
http://www.michigan.gov/mde/0,1607,7-140-6530_6598—,00.html

Minnesota
http://education.state.mn.us/html/intro_support_special_ed.htm

Mississippi
http://www.mde.k12.ms.us/special_education/

Missouri
http://dese.mo.gov/divspeced/

Montana
http://www.opi.state.mt.us/SpecEd/index.html

Nebraska
http://www.nde.state.ne.us/SPED/sped.html

Nevada
http://www.doe.nv.gov/equity/index.html

New Hampshire
http://www.ed.state.nh.us/SpecialEd/special1.htm

New Jersey
http://www.nj.gov/njded/specialed/

New Mexico
http://www.ped.state.nm.us/seo/index.htm

New York
http://www.vesid.nysed.gov/specialed/

North Carolina
http://www.ncpublicschools.org/ec/

North Dakota
http://www.dpi.state.nd.us/speced/index.shtm

Ohio
http://www.ode.state.oh.us/exceptional_children/

Oklahoma
http://sde.state.ok.us/home/defaultie.html

Oregon
http://www.ode.state.or.us/sped/

Pennsylvania
http://www.pde.state.pa.us/special_edu/site/default.asp?g=0&special_eduNav=|978|&k12Nav=|1141|

Rhode Island
http://www.ridoe.net/Special_needs/Default.htm

South Carolina
http://www.myscschools.com/offices/ec/

South Dakota
http://www.state.sd.us/deca/Special/

Tennessee
http://www.state.tn.us/education/speced/index.htm

Texas
http://www.tea.state.tx.us/special.ed/

Utah
http://www.usoe.k12.ut.us/sars/

Vermont
http://www.state.vt.us/educ/new/html/pgm_sped.html

Virginia
http://www.pen.k12.va.us/VDOE/sess/

Washington
http://www.k12.wa.us/SpecialEd/default.aspx

West Virginia
http://wvde.state.wv.us/ose/

Wisconsin
http://www.dpi.state.wi.us/dpi/dlsea/een/

Wyoming
http://www.k12.wy.us/ao/sp/programs/speced.asp

TERRITORIES

Puerto Rico
http://www.nichcy.org/stateshe/pr.htm#specialed

Virgin Islands
http://www.yellowpagesforkids.com/help/vi.htm

Guam
http://www.doe.edu.gu/sped/

Northern Mariana Is.
http://www.pss.cnmi.mp/PSSCentralOffice/index.cfm?pageID=75

ADDITIONAL RESOURCES – NATIONAL

US Department of Education Office of Special Education
http://www.ed.gov/about/offices/list/osers/osep/index.html?src=mr

3 1901 04988 4788